Also by Mindie Barnett

Intermission: How Fervor, Friendships and Faith Took Me to The Second Act

YOU DON'T NEED TO BE A Bitch TO BE A Boss

HOW TO FLAUNT FEMININITY, EMBRACE EMPATHY, AND WIN WITH A VENGEANCE

MINDIE BARNETT

EDITED BY JENICE ARMSTRONG

Post Hill PRESS

A POST HILL PRESS BOOK
ISBN: 978-1-64293-884-5
ISBN (eBook): 978-1-64293-885-2

You Don't Need to Be a Bitch to Be a Boss:
How to Flaunt Femininity, Embrace Empathy, and Win with a Vengeance
© 2021 by Mindie Barnett
All Rights Reserved

Cover art by Cody Corcoran

Post Hill Press
New York • Nashville
posthillpress.com

Published in the United States of America
1 2 3 4 5 6 7 8 9 10

I dedicate this book to all the incredibly talented and driven team members I've had the privilege of working alongside and mentoring through the years at MB and Associates Public Relations and to all the future stars we've yet to see shine. xxx

TABLE OF CONTENTS

Introduction

YOU DON'T SCARE ME

"No person in the world ever lost
anything by being nice to me."

-Lillie Langtry

I am free! Free! Free! Free! On that blustery, cold mid-December Monday morning, I remember thinking that I knew what it must feel like to have been freed from prison. You know—when the inmate first walks out from behind bars, after serving his time, inhales the crisp, clean air into his lungs, and exhales with a sigh that releases fifty pounds of stress and angst. When the ex-con looks up at the blue sky in awe, realizing what it's really like to live again without bars and boundaries. Well, that was me on a Monday morning, about two weeks before Christmas back in 2003. Only my prison had been more like a "country club" penitentiary, because I had had access to fame and lavish luxuries. And lots of catty women. Lots of entitled women. And lots of mean girls. Especially my boss at the time, who I'll call the "Queen Bee"—or "QB" for short.

As I turned a corner inside the Sofitel Hotel in Center City Philadelphia, my pace started to quicken. "Just get me out of here," was all I could think. I didn't even want to look back for fear I'd be sucked backward or into another ugly encounter with QB and her bitchy swarm. I had been engrossed in that hive of hell for the longest six weeks of my life. As the smiling doorman opened the heavy glass doors to let me out, I felt the frigid air on my neck. I tightened my trench coat, pulling it closer to my chest, and hurried out. Walking so quickly, I was close to the rate of a slow jog by the time I reached Rittenhouse Square Park. Before working at QB's public relations firm, I had longed to spend time in that historic park. Sheltered by tall, glitzy apartment buildings and an array of fancy and trendy dining hotspots around its stately parameter, it looked like a postcard photo—especially then, with the gorgeous Christmas tree lit up and shoppers bustling about. But that day, it looked different to me. It was a stark shade of slate and reminded me of anxiety and stress. It was the epicenter of doom and gloom, as my now-former boss's office had a prime spot right next to it. I would cross the gorgeous greenery day in and day out—showing up on many days before dawn and leaving long after dusk. But it wasn't the hours spent working that almost stole my soul. It was the work culture, the climate and aura of fear that made what would appear to be a creative, inspiring position an unbearable form of self-destruction.

Prior to taking this job in public relations, I had spent a decade in journalism. I was a hard-working, respected asset to the stations where I worked. I left a successful broadcasting career to work for this firm, which in that moment, seemed to have been the biggest mistake of my life. That's because QB ran her beehive like a prison. Just walking into the office every morning made my chest tighten. The all-female firm was a group of back-stabbing, manipulative, and self-serving traitors. At first, I was dumbfounded by their treachery. Never in my life had I ever experienced so much ruthlessness. Even in the callous and often cut-throat TV news business, I had never experienced this level of nastiness. I literally could trust no one there. I made the mistake of telling a colleague who had inquired that I had missed working in television news. Within the hour, I was dragged into QB's office—with the same colleague in tow—to explain what I meant by my comment and to say I had no intention of quitting. It was a grilling like no other. The bitch session lasted a full hour.

It wasn't strictly business there either. They would torment me about my personal life too. I once shared with a coworker that I was meeting a guy I had dated after work for dinner. Less than an hour later, the entire office was called into an "emergency" meeting so that I could be quizzed about him—how long I had known him, what he did for a living, where we were going, and more. I felt mocked. Meanwhile, I was on deadline for an important project, and I felt the interaction was flirting with the notion of workplace harassment. I was nearly thirty years old and had already pledged a sorority years prior when I attended

Hofstra University, and here I was being hazed again. That place was ridiculous! I also had no time for it. Workwise or otherwise. I was head and shoulders above this immaturity.

The rule of thumb with QB was that you had to report to work before her no matter how early that was and could never leave the office before she did. She also expected that we come in on weekends and once screamed at me in front of the rest of the team, "I want to see your ass in here on Saturdays. Am I understood? That's all I'll say about that!" So with that, I started adding Saturdays to my already over-flowing work hours. Don't get me wrong. I am not complaining about having to work hard. I'm a first-rate workaholic. I just do not do well working out of fear. I put my all into my assignments because I care about my work, my reputation, my clients, and my good name. I don't work hard because the fear of being fired is looming over my head. I am incredibly driven, competent, and excellent at what I do. QB also didn't lead by example. On most days, she would dash out midday to attend a Pilates class or hit the spa for a facial. She was not ashamed to flaunt her actions either. But we couldn't follow suit. I was the media expert, so my day usually started closer to 6 a.m., with a TV segment or the like. Then, I would work a full day and stay well into the early evening hours, as I had to await QB's departure. In addition, we often had night events and were not expected to leave until they were over.

Believe me, Amanda Priestly had nothing on QB. The work would have been a piece of cake and certainly much more of a pleasure to partake in had she been more of a mentor and less of a monster. Her demeanor, attitude, and personality left much to be desired. Let's just say they were less than motivating. She ran her business with fear. She wanted us to all be scared stiff of her, and we were. She assumed loyalty would be her reward, but she was sorely mistaken. Trying to please her, her team would run to her with secrets. My former colleagues were literally at her beck and call, but it was all for the wrong reasons. They were frightened. They did their day-to-day jobs while looking over their shoulders. No one was friends there. Not true friends, anyways. I vowed to myself I would never run a business like that. Never. Ever. The tension and cruelty were crippling. I hated every second of working for QB. Every. Single. One. Some days, I would dash into the lobby of her office building to take a quick personal call. Sometimes, I just needed to cry. I remember once sobbing uncontrollably to my TV friend, Janet, during one of these two-minute breaks and saying how unhappy I was working there. The doorman had to have heard every word, but I was beyond caring. I had no shame. I needed to get it out. Janet listened intently. She felt sorry for me and knew that although quitting seemed easy to do, it wasn't financially feasible for me to up and quit. I needed to line up another job before leaving this one—but how? I had no time to use the restroom, let alone conduct a job search. Janet warmly consoled me, and I vividly remember how she uttered, "This too shall pass." I felt comfort in her words and knew in time they would ring true. I just needed to stay strong. So, I did.

I started spending my one day a week off from QB job searching—only not in the public relations field. I remember telling myself, "If this is public relations, then I want nothing to do with it." Little did I know how much my life would soon change. Finally, after a few weeks of emails and follow-up calls, I landed a freelance reporter/writer position at the WB station in Philadelphia. It wasn't ideal, as it had no healthcare benefits and work was only available when a reporter would have the day off. But I accepted the position anyway. I figured it was a ticket out of QB hell, as well as a temporary bridge to cross until I figured out my next move.

So, on that freezing December morning, on the day I already fully intended to resign, QB summoned me to the Sofitel. I thought she and I were going to gather for a breakfast meeting as we had before, but when I arrived, I saw the entire team was waiting there with her. I knew that they were about to gang up on me for some minor transgression. Maybe even fire me. But I didn't care because I had a surprise for them! Instead of passively listening to whatever bitch rant QB had planned, as I normally would have, I announced that I was quitting. Just like that, I was out. I could breathe again. My feet could not get me out of there fast enough.

As I raced out of the park and down Locust Street toward the PATCO train I took to and from my New Jersey home, my steps got lighter. I was actually smiling. Had I forgotten how to do that, or were the last six weeks simply so debilitating that my lips had been temporarily paralyzed? Either way, I had my life back. I was back in control of me. No more mean girls. No more bitch boss QB. I vowed I would never put myself through such agony again. No job is worth all of that. No amount of money is worth the price of your dignity. I was talented. I was smart. I had experience. I deserved respect.

As I turned the corner on 16th Street, I saw the stairs to the Speedline entrance and started to descend. I swiped my pass once more to enter the waiting area for the next train. The station was eerily empty—a much different scene than I had just maneuvered two hours before at the height of rush hour. As I boarded my train back to the 'burbs, I rested my head back onto my seat and closed my eyes. For the first time in what seemed like forever, I relaxed. I didn't have a real plan of action in place, but I had myself and trusted that I'd figure it out and somehow end up on top. My thoughts drifted, and I fell into a deep sleep. When I woke up, I realized I had missed my stop. But that was okay. I could just hop on another train and get back to where I started. As I did so, I thought about how sometimes in life, you need to take a step back, even travel backwards a bit, so that you can propel forward. That was me on that day. I had taken a giant step backwards but had no idea about all that was ahead of me. A thriving PR firm, all my own. A talented team to lead and a brand to grow. My poor experiences working for QB helped mold me into becoming the type of leader I am today. I look to inspire, shape, and groom new talent, the stars of tomorrow.

Real leaders mentor; they don't manipulate. You get so much more from employees when you lead with empathy. I believe in educating people about how to perform better. I don't employ fear tactics. Women often struggle with the two extremes. They worry that showing too much compassion makes them look weak when actually, it's just the opposite. Female bosses can be both soft and strong. They can rule without fear and still be the kind of boss employees will want to serve. If you treat your team members right, they'll want to come in early, stay late, and work on a weekend, if necessary. They'll feel and know they're appreciated and valued and, dare I say, may even actually *like* their boss. I'm a firm believer in controlling your work environment and that you can do it without being a bitch.

Chapter 1

DON'T FIGHT THE UNIVERSE

*"Define success on your own terms, achieve it by your
own rules, and build a life you're proud to live."*

–Anne Sweeney, Former President,
Disney ABC Television Group

I did not set out to be an entrepreneur. Quite the contrary. I grew up in a family where a career meant working for someone else. A boss. Someone you answer to and someone who was ultimately responsible for giving you a paycheck. My parents were both educators, and although my dad was a high school principal and ran his school like a CEO, he was not a CEO. He was an employee of the state of New Jersey with a stable income and incredible health benefits. Amazing benefits. He was also set for life with a very cushy pension. One he and our family could count on. He was safe. We were safe. It was normal to us, and it is what I also aspired to have when I began my career. My mom was a teacher with much of the same stability and security, and my younger sister followed suit as well.

I often tell people that I was the "black sheep" of our four-member immediate family because I was the only one who did not pursue a career in education. Instead, I prepared for a career in broadcast journalism, following my calling to write, perform, and connect with the public on so many levels. But even when I was on that career track, I yearned to be financially secure. TV news was far less "safe" than other fields, especially education, but throughout my time in that industry, I worked for big companies with solid healthcare packages, 401k plans, and other perks. I earned a regular paycheck with bonuses if the ratings on my shows were strong, which they often were. So, I got additional income on top of my steady paycheck each quarter. Life was good.

Then, I found myself suddenly unemployed, following my abrupt departure from QB's PR firm. I had lined up regular work at the WB station in Philadelphia reporting as a fill-in, but it was hardly something I could count on for the long term. So, I started aggressively sending out resume tapes to TV stations around the country. Because I had made up my mind that if PR was anything like what I had just experienced, I wanted nothing to do with it. Ever. Never. I was O.U.T.!

One Saturday afternoon, after a much-needed manicure at a salon I'd sometimes frequent in the upscale Philadelphia suburb of Cherry Hill, I wandered into a new boutique adjacent to the spa. I had never seen it before. The walls were a dark rustic rouge color, and the lighting was dim. Beautiful, expensive clothing lined the perimeter like fine artwork. I wandered around slowly and fell instantly in love with the store's gorgeous, exquisite display of fashion at its finest. The labels on the clothing were designer names I recognized. If I had had the budget, I would have purchased one of everything! The store was called "Changes," an odd name I thought for a women's apparel boutique, but the owner explained that she had just rebranded and had taken a partner, hence the name. Although the selection was incredible, the store was vacant. Not a soul was in there that day, other than me and the owner, who must have been thrilled to have company. She chatted me up, asking, where did I live? (At the time with my parents in Medford.) Was I married? (Nope.) What did I do for a living? I explained to her that I was a news anchor/reporter and left the field to pursue public relations but had quit that job after only six weeks due to the unhealthy work environment, and that I was looking for a permanent TV position. She said, "How interesting!" Then, the well-dressed, nicely perfumed, perfectly made-up platinum blonde shared, "I'm in need of a publicist. We just interviewed with a firm in Philadelphia, but they were much too expensive. I wonder if you could help me?" I responded, "Well, I honestly don't know how long I will be in the area." I wanted to be as honest as possible with her and not take on something I couldn't fulfill. "I think I could help you for a few months as long as you understand that I may need to leave before our time is up," I explained. She was perfectly fine with that arrangement. And just like that, I became an entrepreneur. It was really that easy.

I came up with an obscenely low monthly fee because I had not yet realized my real value or worth and drew up a one-page agreement stating my responsibilities, the intended deliverables to the storeowner, and, of course, when my fee was to be paid. Since I didn't have a real company, the checks were simply written out to me. (Not the best idea when launching a business, FYI!) Incidentally, the income I got from the boutique, coupled with the money I was earning at the WB TV news station, was the same amount as the salary I had been making at QB's company. So, at least my finances were in a good place for the time being.

It was time for me to get down to work. I have always had an incredibly strong work ethic, and now more than ever, I wanted to shine and shine bright. Now, remember, it was December. And, what happens that time of year? People shop. They shop a lot! They shop for their friends; they shop for their families; they shop for their coworkers and even for themselves. And she was my one and only client at the time, and if nothing else, I am, and always have been, super aggressive. So, what do you think happened? You've got it! This little store, the one that almost no one had heard of, began to be seen everywhere. I pitched that store to everyone I could think of, and it paid off. *The Philadelphia Daily News* did an entire holiday shopping feature on the Changes boutique. The local NBC station produced a live segment showcasing beautiful models wearing trendy holiday looks from the store. A reporter from the local Fox station's "Good Day, Philadelphia!" program did a live shot one morning right from the store featuring party dresses. The list of press placements that month went on and on. Suddenly, my client's once-vacant store was packed. Positioned by my PR efforts as the "it" place to shop, women in search of high-end looks flocked in. Her credit card machine was in overdrive, and everyone kept asking her, "How are you everywhere?"

Luckily for me, the boutique owner wasn't quiet about what I had done for her business. She was kind enough to share my new role and how much I had contributed to her marketing and branding success. Also, luckily for me, some high-profile women from the community were customers of hers. One was the wife of the owner of a massive retail chain, who insisted that her husband needed to meet me. So, my client gave her my information, and in less than a week, I was sitting across from him, in his office, discussing a PR campaign for his group of fifteen stores. Within about an hour, the Forman Mills empire was my second client. Was this for real?

Then, one day, I was at my go-to hair salon for a chop and fresh highlights. No matter where I was living—a dorm in college, away working in Louisiana or Illinois—I always came home for my highlights and haircuts. On this particular day in late January, I was sitting in my stylist's chair when the owner who I've known since high school walked over to find out which TV station I was working for. Many who had known me much of my news career often found it compelling to catch up on my latest professional endeavor whenever I was in town. When I explained that I had taken a temporary leave and was doing some PR consulting, he shared, "That's funny. We are actually in need of a publicist! Make an appointment to meet with me on Monday." So, I did, and two days later, Bernard's Salon & Spa of Cherry

Hill (and later Marlton too) became my third client. (I later learned that I had beaten out a very established PR firm for that gig!)

A few weeks later, a dear friend of mine from TV news set up a meeting for me and her husband, who had opened a skate park in Philadelphia and needed public relations support. Soon after, his business, Title 10 Skatepark, became my fourth client. Still no formal company formed. Still no real business name selected. Checks still written to me personally. Still not fully understanding the magnitude of what was unfolding. My "company" was swiftly growing, blossoming, really. Yes, I put in a ton of hard work and always brought my "A" game, but that is how I always did things. In school, in news, in life. I never under-delivered. I always over-delivered. Always viewed any work mission as "paying my dues," and I always strived to please and perform. Always. Always. Always. Now, here is a little secret that I don't often share when telling reporters, interns, or whomever asks me about how I launched MB and Associates: I really didn't want to do it. At least, not initially. In my mind, MB was just a means to an end. A way to pay my bills until a "real" job came along. Let me be crystal clear: I loved what I was doing. I just couldn't see past my own vision of going back into TV news. I'd apply and land meetings with news directors at very prominent outlets but to no avail. Often, when I'd be at a station to oversee a client's segment, the news director (who is essentially the CEO in a newsroom) would agree to meet with me after the segment was over. (And my client had departed the premises.) We'd talk about whatever on-air position was available at the time and about my skills, and they'd conduct an informal job interview with me. I was really, really close to securing a handful of decent on-air positions at these stations. I almost landed the role as host of a lifestyle midday show at one of the big stations in town. I also was a runner-up for an investigative reporter position at an all-news cable network in the city and a handful of other solid reporting or anchoring jobs in markets near Philadelphia. But not one came through. None. It was beyond frustrating. Thankfully, I had my PR work to keep me beyond busy, but I'd constantly think to myself, "Why doesn't the universe want me to get another news job?" I even remember looking up to the sky one day and asking, "Why!?" It's like that saying, "God's plans for you are better than any plans you have for yourself." That quote is spot on. I didn't see it or understand it back then, but I realize it now—establishing MB and Associates was my destiny. Period. Everything happens for a reason. Everything!

By spring, I had about six clients and a new boyfriend. Life was humming along. And then, I got a phone call from a news director in Scranton, PA, which is known in the news industry as a feeder market to Philadelphia. It was two hours from home—not commutable, but also not so far that I couldn't come home most weekends or holidays that I was off. It was a main anchor position and included daily reporting. The money was decent, and it came with all of the benefits and perks often associated with corporate America. I was at a crossroads. What to do? I wanted to take it. The PR gig, after all, was supposed to be just a holding place for me until something more structured and substantial came along, and here it was. It finally had arrived.

But now I was unsure if I still wanted it. I had interviewed and auditioned for this position back in January. I thought things had gone very well when the news director asked for my reference list. Then, a day or so later, he called to tell me that although he had planned to hire me, he had gotten word that his budget had been cut drastically, and, therefore, he had been forced to "freeze" the position. See, I told you, while so many opportunities were close, I just hadn't been able to seal the deal. But this time, I had the job if I wanted it. I told the news director I needed a day to think things over. He was a little surprised, given my eagerness a few months prior, but agreed to give me some time to ponder. I discussed things with my parents, who were supportive of whichever direction I wanted to take, but felt the news path was likely safer and more secure for me.

Then, I discussed the situation with my boyfriend (who became my husband and is now my ex-husband), and he saw things differently. Not only was he concerned with the distance and the difficulty of maintaining a serious relationship some 120-miles apart, he also couldn't fathom why I'd be willing to abandon my business. "I can't believe you're just going to walk away from your company," he said one afternoon as we sat on his sofa. "What company?" I asked in confusion. "Your company, Mindie! You have a business! You're doing very well, and your clients are counting on you." That was a profound turning point for me. Sometimes you need trusted confidants to point out a picture that remains blurry in your own view. With great pause I considered what he was saying. I had never taken the PR "business" seriously until that afternoon sitting in his loft weighing out my career options and praying I'd pick the best path. But after he spoke up, something inside of me clicked. I decided in that moment that I would give it a shot. If the PR business wound up falling apart, I would go back into news.

So, with that, MB and Associates Public Relations was born. I met with an attorney. I set up my LLC, The Barnett Group, in April of 2004 but will always use the anniversary date of December 15, 2003 as the year MB was founded, since that was when I actually began establishing myself as a successful, independent publicist. My journey was a little backwards, but I think it was meant to work out this way. When I went to open my business bank account, it was much less daunting not having to deposit part of my savings into the business, as I already had a pretty lucrative cash-flow from the roster of clients I was working with. I already had work to tackle. I didn't need to go seek it out. I was ahead by leaps and bounds as compared to other entrepreneurs just launching a company. Now, I needed to maintain what I already had and grow the business. That's far less stressful than hoping you will secure customers or clientele. So, while backwards, this unusual track really propelled me forward and much faster than I could ever have anticipated!

Now, seventeen years later as I write this, MB and Associates is soaring further than I ever could have imagined on that spring day almost two decades ago. It hasn't always been smooth sailing. I've had my fair share of storms to weather. I have been turned upside down—during one low period, I actually contemplated folding. But with lots of passion, perseverance, and persistence, my company withstood the crash of 2008, the birth of (and life struggles associated with) two babies, a divorce and life reshuffling, financial setbacks due to business ebbs and flows, and five offices before finally buying a two-story condo in the Greater Philadelphia region, where MB is now based. Add to that a home office in Manhattan and clients not only in New York City and Philadelphia but all over the country. MB has and still is doing superbly well. It has been my greatest gift (after my children, of course), and I love MB with all my heart and soul.

After nearly two decades, we have become nationally acclaimed, and I have had the honor of training, grooming, and working alongside dozens of employees over the course of the years. They have all taught me something along the way too. How to be more patient; how to be more communicative; why it is important to not always fix their problems; and how to look at issues from a fresh perspective. I owe much of my success to their invaluable contributions. Together, we have conquered, learned from mistakes along the way, and leaned on one another until it was time to part ways. I can honestly say that I have not only had a hand in branding and creating household names for my clients but that I have also had a role in molding and shaping the successful careers for so many who have come through the doors of MB and Associates. Both are blessings, both are equally rewarding, and both clear the way for prosperity. I feel so lucky to have had (and still have) the rare opportunity to have such an impact on another's growth. I never take it for granted.

My first MB and Associates office was actually in the third bedroom of my boyfriend's house. It was very makeshift and consisted primarily of a separate landline to use as my firm's official office number, a desk, and my laptop. Once I became engaged and ultimately married, I made it more "mine" in terms of the décor and setup. But I hated working from home. I found it hard to separate work from life and would constantly feel drawn to that space at all hours. Every day. All day. It was not healthy. I also craved human connection. My boyfriend, who worked as a jeweler in Philadelphia, would leave at the crack of dawn and not return until the end of the workday. So, on days that I didn't have a shoot or a client meeting to attend, I would be alone all day long. I work best in collaborative settings, where I have others to run ideas by in real-time and in person. As you can imagine, the working-from-home "new normal" that became a necessity during the pandemic wasn't ideal for me in the least either. In fact, other than being able to see my children day in and day out, there was no other appealing factor to me about the WFH situation. Simply put, I hated working away from people. So, it was very evident that I would need to invest in an office sooner rather than later. Luckily the sooner arrived faster than I imagined. When it came time to hire my first employee (albeit she was part-time and more of an assistant to me), I knew it was time to set up shop in an official office out of the house.

At the time I was representing the incredibly fashionable Leehe Fai Goldfarb, who owned an exquisite women's apparel boutique just off of Rittenhouse Square in Philadelphia. That neighborhood was the Mecca of fashion for women in the city. I was in heaven. It was so fun working with her. Leehe's creativity and implementation of in-store events and shopping parties always gave me amazing content to pitch the fashion writers and feature reporters. I organized the details for events, secured media around it, and was on-site to mingle and network with the many notables who attended. In addition, I secured regular TV and other monthly media placements. Leehe was well-connected in the city, and I was privy to many new business contacts just by having her store on my resume. In addition, she had a vacant office she was looking to rent on Walnut Street, a stone's throw from the prestigious Rittenhouse Square area. She had attained a suite and only needed one of the three spaces. So we worked out a sublet and rent arrangement, and I was on my way.

Center City it was! I always loved the city—still do. I am a city girl through and through, and with half of my clients based in Philadelphia at the time and most of the media I was working with also there, it made sense that I be there too. My first office was pure perfection. Literally in the heart of the city—where you'd want to see and be seen. I loved it! I would be so energized just driving into town for work each morning, walking the streets for some fresh air, and taking in the sights when grabbing lunch. It was simply good for my soul. And my assistant loved it too. We'd have morning meetings, go over the priorities of the day, and conspire and inspire one another to be more.

Her name was Kelie, and she was fantastic. A stay-at-home mom to twins, she was itching to get back into work life again and had some PR experience from her career before motherhood. It was a perfect fit. She was loyal and hardworking and wanted to see me do well. I taught her all about news, showed her how to pitch a story effectively, and (I believe) gave her a new lease on life. We were great for one another. I also attribute one of my most rewarding PR projects to the wit of Kelie. One early spring day, as she strolled in, dressed to the nines, with her Starbucks coffee in tow, she pranced right into my corner office and tossed a magazine down, right in front of my face. "Min! We can help her," she enthusiastically announced. She swiftly thumbed through that week's issue of *In Touch* magazine to show me a dramatic story about a young woman who went skydiving, but her parachute didn't deploy, and she was sent freefalling through the sky, ending in a crash landing head-first onto the pavement. She broke nearly every bone in her body, dismantling her face and knocking out her teeth. The woman was Shayna Richardson (now West), and this story was a follow-up to a series of other stories this publication (along with nearly every other national outlet) did on her ordeal. This story was sharing her reveal, her new face, and the fact that she found out she was pregnant. Not only was it a miracle that she survived such a deadly blow, but her unborn baby did too. She was proclaiming her incredible gratitude to the doctors who pieced her back together and also shared her sadness about her smile in this update story. She was saying how she had once been known for her perfect teeth and now she would be forced to wear false teeth for the rest of her life.

At the time, MB was representing a world-renowned periodontist, celebrated for his extreme talent in implant procedures, Dr. Alan Meltzer. Kelie suggested we approach Dr. Meltzer and see if he would be willing to donate his time and materials to give Shayna a new smile. A permanent one. A smile to replicate the once she once had. I told Kelie to contact the reporter at the magazine and explain our idea and see if she would be willing to share Shayna's direct contact information. In the meantime, I approached Dr. Meltzer and advocated passionately for what would become a mass media opportunity for him, as well as a chance for him to make a difference in a young woman's life. It was a win-win situation. After a variety of phone conversations with Dr. Meltzer and diligent research from Kelie, we made the connection. In less than four weeks, Shayna was on a flight to New Jersey from her home in Joplin, Missouri. I picked her and her mother up at the airport and brought them to Dr. Meltzer. This routine went on over the course of several months, as she would travel in (via Dr. Meltzer's generosity) and have various procedures done. In the end, she got her smile. A gorgeous, stunning set of teeth that look exactly like the ones she was once so proud of. And Dr. Meltzer received national accolades and media coverage. We pitched every outlet that ever covered her story in the past and added to the list. The dental donation was covered on the *Today Show*, *Good Morning America*, *Entertainment Tonight*, *Inside Edition*, and *The Oprah Winfrey Show*…just to name a few. And as for me, I walked away with a major career accomplishment, a full heart, and a new friend. Shayna and I are still in touch and speak from time to time. That was my second year in business, and that project remains in my mind as one of my most rewarding PR projects of all time.

Even to this day, (aside from the part of my week when I work in Manhattan), my favorite office address was the one I had in Philadelphia. But after a little over a year, I knew it was time to go. I was growing, and I needed to hire another employee. I needed more space and it made sense, economically and personally, to leave the city. At that point of my life, I was married, and since my husband and I lived in New Jersey and planned to start a family in the near future, I reluctantly decided it was best to pick a spot on the other side of the bridge back in the suburbs. But somewhere I could still feel a city vibe: in the downtown environment of Haddonfield.

Ironically, this was the town in which I would catch the Speedline train rides when working in QB's office. Heading to the station, I used to drive down Main Street and admire all the adorable shops, which would be dark and closed at that wee hour of the morning, and think how charming the town was. I never really knew much of Haddonfield growing up, but going to and from it daily back then gave me a real appreciation for how charming and vibrant it was. I met with a real estate agent, saw some available spaces, and took a two-room flat on the second floor of a quaint storefront just off the main drag of Kings Highway. It was perfect. I had my own office and my two employees shared the adjacent room. Kelie remained part-time because that was all her hectic schedule could allow, but the other employee, Jane (and if you read my first book you know all about Jane and her psychopathic personality, compulsive lying, and back-stabbing, which I will not get into in this book, but it's shared in great detail in *Intermission: How Fervor, Friendships and Faith Took Me to the Second Act*) was the new addition. The office was cheery, and I painted the space a sunshine yellow and my office a lavender purple, which boasted a hand-painted floral mural an artist friend of mine created. And I hung a white chandelier straight above my executive desk. Every office I've ever had has had chandeliers. It has become a trademark of sorts.

At about this time, we were growing rapidly and becoming even more well-known in the marketplace. I no longer was only receiving referrals from clients and people who knew me personally but was vetting many cold calls from prospective clients who had heard of my name or done an online search for Philadelphia-based PR firms. Another perk to all the press we were obtaining weekly was the organic way search engine optimization can grow. Because we were digitally attached to all the news placements our clients got, we were bumped up in Google's algorithm. That is substantial, considering how many companies pay a great deal of money to achieve what we were able to organically. Some of the most flattering referrals were the ones that came from the press itself. One such case involved a well-known editor at *Philadelphia Magazine* sharing my contact information with the head of marketing at Tiffany & Co., Northeast. They were looking for a PR firm to spearhead campaigns at their Center City Philadelphia store, King of Prussia location, and store in Atlantic City. They contacted this senior editor to offer recommendations based on working relationships they had with area agencies. Mine was one of the three considered. It was incredibly exciting. The Tiffany & Co. brand is not only elite and incredibly reputable, but I was also a devout fan and customer of the jewelry and accessories since college, and their name on my resume alone would push my company faster and further than I could ever imagine.

The courting process to get their work was brutal. I had a series of phone calls to start, during which I was grilled and asked a variety of marketing questions, quizzed about my knowledge of the brand and the various differences in the three locations I would be working on. Then, I needed to create a very formal and lengthy proposal. I spent days on it. I needed to have multiple copies of this mini book made, bound, and hand-delivered to the team of five from New York City who came down to the Bellevue Hotel in Center City, where the flagship regional store was located, to interview me. They were kind but cold, and I felt a bit out of place because of that. I was dressed well. I had a beautiful skirt suit on, a fresh blowout, and Chanel pumps. I looked great. I sounded great, but I don't think at the time I had the high-end presence the brand needed. My ideas were solid, my press clips were top-notch but, in the end, they went in another direction. My take-home was that I had some more polishing to do. Polishing of myself. If I wanted to work and grow into the high-end, upper echelon of clientele, then I needed to present as such. Even if I wasn't exactly in that ballpark yet. Image is everything in public relations. Lucky for me, I've always has a flair for fashion and never batted an eyelash at spending my hard-earned money on an overly expensive pair of shoes, bag, or coat. So, that part was easy. I just needed to hone my demeanor, learn the lay of the land a bit more, and morph into what I wanted to eventually represent. In time, that became my reality. I learned how to walk the walk and talk the talk. I wasn't being inauthentic, I just evolved. I grew and I blossomed.

Despite this minor Tiffany & Co. hiccup, my firm grew swiftly that first year in Haddonfield. I landed my first surgical client (who's still with me, by the way), a famous regional bakery, a new salon and spa, and also landed some special events. My work life was just zipping along. I was coaching my team of two, and they were proving to be tremendous assets. (At that time, Jane was committed to her role as an MB publicist and had the interest of the company at heart, at least that's what I thought.) We were cultivating more national contacts, still mainly focusing on Philadelphia, but as my client roster grew, some of our experts warranted the national spotlight on a regular basis. We cultivated stronger relationships with producers at TV shows like *Inside Edition, Good Morning America,* and *The Howard Stern Show* that year.

My next real estate move was to a much bigger office, right in the center of town, where I now employed two full-time employees and took on my first-ever college intern, Jenna Stark. You'll read about Jenna later on and all of her incredible career accomplishments. She and I remain extremely close, and I now lean on her as much or more as she once leaned on me to learn the ropes of PR. A year after moving to that second Haddonfield office, I became a mother and started the insanely hectic, stressful, and rewarding working mom balancing act. It was hard. It was grueling and some days downright unbearable, and just as I thought I was in a (sort of) groove, the housing crash of 2008 hit, and I lost a quarter of my clientele. The first client to go was the salon I was working with at the time. I saw the writing on the wall months before, though. They had been paying me on time, but when I would go to deposit their monthly check, within days, I'd receive notice that it had bounced. Not only was I now in need of the funds owed me for the past month of service, but I needed to seek reimbursement for the bank fee that I was hit with. It was incredibly infuriating. Clearly, they were in financial trouble, so when they shared that they could no longer support my PR efforts, I wasn't surprised and let them out of their contract. The next one to terminate their agreement was the women's apparel boutique I had been representing in Haddonfield. The store was extremely upscale, featuring designers like Escada, Moschino, and Pamella Roland. Filled with mostly dresses and elite suit wear, when the economy sank, they felt a major blow. Unable to make ends meet, and after the owner let me go, a few short months later she had to close her doors. Awful. And there were a few other sad stories similar to that one. A restaurant who was hurting financially and a furrier who was no longer in the black. It was a bleak time. Nonessential purchases like designer dresses and jeans, fancy spa treatments, and big jewelry were few and far between for the average person. My lifestyle clients were hurting. They couldn't afford PR anymore, and so I was forced to pivot. I began focusing on medicine and professional service industries like finance and law. It was a godsend. Representing experts from those fields has enabled my firm to shine above much of our competition. These types of clients have proven to be incredibly lucrative and have given me a real sense of importance. I transitioned from pitching fluffy (yet fun) shopping or beauty segments to also offering tried-and-true "news you can use" to audiences. I created a new niche for myself and my firm. I left the parties and more social and soft aspects of public relations to the other firms. I carved out a brand for MB, which positioned us as the pinnacle for real news story coverage, at a fast pace and not just in the local news but on the national level. We were flying! Today, we still have a pocket of lifestyle clientele, but it's the doctors and professional service experts that I proactively seek to work with time and time again.

Back to packing boxes. After four years of calling Haddonfield home for MB, we needed to move again. This time, because my daughter was entering preschool and the triangular commute I was making from home to work to her school and back was taking up too much of my valuable time. So, into the Main Street complex in Voorhees we went. This office was in a pretty promenade setting. It didn't have the same flair of downtown Haddonfield, but the office layout was more desirable, and my daughter's school was across the parking lot. I now had four full-time employees: three publicists and my first-ever full-time assistant, as well as two interns. Having an assistant was a life changer for me. Her name was Jaclyn, and she was an aspiring publicist. She helped me with my day-to-day tasks and learned the ropes of PR as she went. I'd take the time to explain to her what I was doing, why I was asking her to complete various tasks, and would correct her when she was in error. We were a great team. And I was able to do my job as a publicist and CEO so much more effectively with her support. My publicist employees were incredible too. Dana was a former TV producer and could think on her feet and come up with ideas in a pinch; Caron also came from a TV news background and was always looking to troubleshoot and collaborate with me, which I always appreciated (Caron is still a member of the MB team today); Meryl, who was very green upon coming aboard, had turned into a very positive force in the office and was adored by the clients she served. I was so lucky! I steered the ship with loose ropes, never yanking or pulling too hard. I created much of my management style during that time. I shared with the team my desire for everyone to deliver swift and consistent results and explained tactics to achieve such success.

They were receptive, they were eager to grow, and were never afraid to speak up whenever they had a difference of opinion. I was and always will be an open-minded leader. I never pretend to have all the answers. Even if I think I know the answer, it doesn't mean it's always the right solution. Just like in news, when multiple eyes are on a script before a story makes air, I believe the more ideas brought into the mix, the better the chances of success. I always welcomed competing opinions, and I wholeheartedly believe that mindset has created a workplace for my team to flourish as a company and as individuals.

Because I was so hands-on with my team, dedicating any and all opportunities that arose as a time to teach, I was creating a well-oiled machine. I am and always have been extremely hands-on and spend much of my time in the weeds, in the line of fire, with the rest of the group, but I was starting to let go of the reins from time to time—if only for a few hours once a week—and spend some time away from the office. I initially dedicated Mondays as a work-from-home day so that I could be with my daughter, Arielle, after her core day at school. I also found that this small amount of time away enabled my team to have more independence without me in the next room. They were able to bond with one another more freely and think on their feet in my absence. And they knew if a fire erupted, I was a simple phone call away, and if really necessary, a ten-minute drive to the office. It was just enough for both me and them.

When summer came around, I took things a little further, adding Fridays to my Monday work-from-home routine and worked remotely from my summer home at the Jersey shore. I enrolled my daughter in a summer camp those two days at a temple in Ventnor City to add to the other three days she attended day camp back home. We would hit the road after dinner Thursday nights and settle in before her bedtime. Then, Friday mornings, I would drive her to her camp and set up shop in my kitchen, where I'd work until it was time to pick her up around noon. During her naptime, I'd get more work taken care of until she woke up at about 2 p.m. Then, we would hit the beach and spend time alone before my husband would drive down to have dinner with us. We would enjoy the weekend together at the beach, and he'd leave to head back to our home by early evening on Sunday. I repeated the camp/work routine on Monday, but instead of hitting the beach after her nap, I'd hit the road and get home in time for dinner. Then, back to the office on Tuesday. It was a great summer!

This routine didn't go on past that season, but it was really freeing to me to have been able to spend some quality time (even if the majority of it was near a laptop) out of the office and with my toddler. Because I never took a maternity leave (I literally gave birth midweek and went back to the office the following Monday!), I was starting to feel as if I had sold myself out on those special, tender moments that can never be recouped. This arrangement didn't make up for the lost time I traded in to run my company, but these few days at the shore with her did ease the pang in my heart a bit. I had my incredible team to thank for allowing me to have this freedom that many other entrepreneurs take for granted.

That was my only real time working regularly from home, other than during the pandemic when most non-essential workers worked remotely. These days, I spend an extra hour or two in the morning catching up on invoices or bookkeeping and use that time to do deep work, without distractions. However, I split most weeks between New Jersey and Manhattan. While I'm working with clients and media in New York City, my team is feverishly holding down the headquarters' workload in my absence. It's a different team (all but Caron, of course) from what I had back then, but they're my most prized asset. Without them, I'd never be able to accomplish what I can day in and day out.

After five years and one more baby (my son Julian), I decided it was time to change addresses yet again. By the way, and I'm sure anyone who's done it will attest, moving a business is ten-fold more involved and stressful than moving a residence. All the essentials needed to conduct business have to be set up in less than twenty-four hours. It's an utter nightmare. This time around, I wasn't hiring more employees and I wasn't looking to shorten my commute to and from preschool. My lease was up, the rent was going up, and I was starting to feel like I was tossing away money with each rent payment.

I was always extremely conservative with my income, paying myself a decent salary but never anything over-the-top. Always looking over my shoulder for the next rainstorm, I had saved up a nice nest egg just in case things got slow. I had accumulated enough for a very substantial down payment on a commercial property. I had always loved the Pavilions of Greentree in Marlton. I once represented an aesthetic medicine doctor who had an office in that complex. The units were all two-stories and very modern. In addition, this professional complex sits in a prime location. It's a hop, skip, and a jump to Philadelphia and also close to the New Jersey Turnpike, as well as to trains and buses that go to New York City (where I was starting to frequent for work almost monthly). It was also a ten-minute commute to my home, now in Mount Laurel. Although I did look at other properties, this was really my only choice. But none were available. And just as I had resigned to sign another lease and try again in a few years, my agent called. He had personally walked into each unit and asked the owners if they had any intention of selling at some point in the near future. One insurance broker was planning to retire and expressed interest in selling. So, the unit MB now calls home was never even listed on the market. I bought it as is, gutted the place, and created the most exquisite environment to create and conquer!

I had hardwood floors installed, redid the bathroom, kitchen area, my office, the lobby area, conference room, and the loft, where most of my team is located. There are, of course, numerous chandeliers throughout, along with other crystal light fixtures lining the perimeter, winter-white walls, dark wood accents, hints of cobalt blue, grey tones, and my office is coated in blush peach and ivory. I'm so proud of the space I created, and I know my team feels pride in coming to this office too. It has been the backdrop for many photo shoots (MTV has even shot in my office!) and the site for more television interviews than I can count. What's more, it's all mine—well, the commercial real estate company I set up to make the purchase is mine (as well as my children's). I now have a property to leave to them one day. Something they can use, rent, whatever they choose to do. It was one of the wisest investments I've made and another one of the ongoing gifts MB has given me.

Just as we were starting to settle in, I received a phone call from a news colleague of mine. He had been an anchor/reporter at News 12 New Jersey for about a year when I was reporting there and went on to UPN9, now WPIX11 in New York. He had since left television news and was the CEO of a media consulting company and had a client he thought I could help. The client was a psychologist who had a special interest in politics. He was trying to brand himself as a political psychologist and someone the media may turn to for body language translation and analysis during debates and such. The expert was based in New York and also had a home in Naples, Florida. Although New York would have been a stronger fit, given the plethora of national news outlets, securing regular media exposure in the Fort Myers tele-vision market was his main priority. I didn't have a strong footprint in that region at the time, but that never stopped me before and it didn't this time. Cultivating new media relationships brought me an adrenaline rush much like the thrill of a racecar driver screeching through a turn. (I'm not kidding.) Gaining the media's attention and getting them to trust you and work with you regularly is not an easy feat and something I find personal pleasure in. So, Fort Myers it was, and in a short time (and after much persistence on our end) we had created solid relationships with members of the assignment desks, show producers, and on-air talent at all the affiliate stations.

One station in particular (and the leader in ratings in that media market) had a regular segment focusing on politics. The segment was aired live during the morning newscast and often repeated (live-to-tape) in the evening show. We had been booking our expert frequently, and it was becoming apparent how much the viewers enjoyed his involvement. I had an idea. Maybe they'd consider paying him and giving him a "contributor" title. Having worked in media markets similar in size, I knew the money wouldn't be much, but the title alone would be worth it. So, I reached out to the station's news director and suggested my idea. I painted the picture in his view, though. I explained how having a regular contributor would be a great asset to his already esteemed team and that we'd offer exclusivity if my client could obtain a weekly segment (with more as needed) in exchange for payment and an official role at the station. After many unanswered emails and phone calls, the news boss finally got back to me and was keen on discussing it. I flew to Florida to meet with him and see the station first-hand. And before I left, my client had a deal. I negotiated the contract, worked out the terms, and helped create his local, household name in that community.

That was the first client contract I spearheaded. My second involved a celebrity pro-ball player. A former Philadelphia Eagle and football legend in the city. He had been my client for a few years when he started thinking he should be getting paid for his on-air work. I agreed. The region loved him, and when he appeared on the air, the ratings for those newscasts definitely soared. So, without knowing what opportunities may even exist, I started reaching out to management at some of the stations where we'd book him most often. As luck would have it, the ABC station in Philadelphia was revamping their Sunday night football show, which followed the Sunday football game carried on the network. They were interested in talking to see if my client would be a fit to co-host with their well-known and ultra-famous sports anchor. I went to the station, met with the sports team, took more meetings with the promotions department, and negotiated with the station's general manager. This was a much bigger station and much more intimidating than the one in Fort Myers, as Philadelphia is the country's fourth largest market in the United States and this station was owned and operated by the ABC Network. It was big time. But I did it! I was a pro. I got my client a great deal and gained even more respect from the top management at the station. They already enjoyed working with me, but now they were sharing how much they loved my demeanor and dedication to making sure both sides were able to work well with one another and feel enthusiastic about the partnership. Maybe I missed my calling as an agent!

About two years after the finishing touches were put onto the MB Marlton office, I decided it was time to also take on Manhattan and set up shop there too. It is no secret that I've always had a mad passion for the Big Apple and slowly but surely was acquiring more clients there. Not to mention, many of the national shows we were working with are based in New York. The year was 2017, and I was newly divorced, sharing custody of my two children with their father and living in Voorhees, not far from where I once had an office. The timing was right. I had more time to spend away from home now, since I didn't need to be in New Jersey every day for the kids. But rather than lease an office, I chose to take an apartment and use it as a home office by day and as a fun bachelorette pad by night. Another incredible decision both professionally and personally!

Professionally, having a Manhattan address enabled me to be taken more seriously by Manhattan media and national outlets. Prospective clients also liked the fact that I was local and were more inclined to hire me. The clients I was gaining made this extremely large extra business expense worth every penny. Personally, I was living my best life. On the days and nights I didn't have my kids with me, I was able to live a more carefree existence. I reconnected with old friends and formed deeper connections with new ones. New York City no longer intimidated me. I was now one with so many movers and shakers there and thriving. I still am! I'm now in a new apartment, in a nicer section of town and even more engrossed with the city and the many influential people who live and work there. MB has definitely made its mark on Manhattan and continues to make a lasting imprint.

The list of clients and press we've worked with since making New York City our second home is too long to name, but I shall share two amazing projects we work on annually for our ultra-high-end celebrity French stylist, Julien Farel. Julien and his sophisticated and super smart wife, Suelyn, run the incredibly reputable and impressive Julien Farel Restore Salon & Spa on the Upper East Side. Julien is the go-to for many A-list celebrities and has become the pinnacle for hair and beauty on the national level. He was not in need of PR to put his name on the map but was in need of support and someone to add to the already regular press queries he gets. I was exhilarated when he shared that he and Suelyn had decided to hire me.

One of the most exciting projects I had (and still have) the honor of helping with is his involvement in New York Fashion Week. The salon is often the designated creative team for the beauty side of the Dennis Basso show, among others, and one or two of my team and I get to work the entire event backstage, often with the celebrity models and A-list superstars who walk the runway. I invite and host reporters from outlets like *Vogue, The Cut, The Zoe Report* and more as they interview Julien and take snapshots of the models getting primped for the catwalk. Then, we watch the show in its entirety, side-by-side with the highest of fashion press you can think of. It's electric. It's a ton of work. My feet usually ache at the end of the day, and more times than I can count, I've nearly lost my lunch from stress, but each and every show I am mesmerized by the mere fact I am there, with a backstage press pass, working this enormously profound event. It's like a dream.

Another surreal annual project we work on with Julien Farel is the US Open. Julien's salon has been the official salon of the US Open for thirteen years and counting. Each year, he and his esteemed team set up shop right in the training facility at Arthur Ashe Stadium. It's a very elite area. Only the tennis greats, their trainers, and their spouses are permitted access, in addition to the JF team and the MB team, of course. We are given exclusive passes to enter the building and work one-on-one with every tennis great you can imagine. We also get a bird's eye view of the practice area and are able to have lunch in their dining facility (which is nothing short of incredible!). Our role is to pitch and escort media—both local and national—into the salon area to interview Julien and capture the tennis pros getting haircuts, manicures, and more. All the press who come to cover the matches are also in need of feature stories, and this is ideal on many levels. Again, lots and lots of time on my feet, more running around than one would ever imagine an indoor salon shoot would warrant, and many last-minute changes and live shot issues later. This is by far one of my favorite annual events. I feel incredibly blessed to be a part of it. Merci beaucoup, Suelyn and Julien!

My intention is to grow in New York as MB turns twenty. Our headquarters will likely always remain in Marlton, but my plan is to soon have an employee based in Manhattan. That will be our next full-time hire, as I think having someone to work regularly alongside me there will give us even more of a footprint and more credibility with our clients, as well as the Manhattan media.

As I brace myself for my fiftieth birthday in three more years, I'm trying to plan intelligently. The pace of PR is fast. The track is slick. The pressure is intense. And the hustle is hard. I love what I do. It's embedded in my soul, but I know life is also short, so I'm looking at my team as the future of MB now more than ever. I will always lead my company but am working to let go a little at a time so that I can enable others to lead as well. With careful guidance and patience, I know they have the talent and ability to do so.

Manhattan will also always be a permanent address for MB too. And, in time, I will also have a third location. Somewhere I will set up shop personally and professionally half of the year. Preferably somewhere warm! Likely southern Florida. (Although I also have an obsession with Los Angeles.) In either case, I intend to spend most of my time in the newest location during the winter and spring and spend my time in Manhattan and Marlton during the summer and fall. So, I'll be leaning heavily on my team as the years go by. Letting them take the reins, a little bit more at a time.

As I age and the company turns older too, my team will be the future of MB with me as the foundation of support, never letting the ship sink. I know I have set the tone for a workplace full of enlightenment, encouragement, and empathy for one another, for the media, for the clients we serve. The MB team will also have a hand in shaping the rock stars of tomorrow—as I have a hand in molding the leaders of today. I also plan to focus my energy in upcoming years inspiring women to be more confident, support one another, and understand that just because another has a full plate doesn't mean there isn't enough food for you. Too many women are so focused on looking over their shoulders, they miss what's staring them right in the mirror. Their own beautiful face.

Trust the Universe and Give in to Your Gut!

✓ *Create a clear view of what you wish to unfold. Then, you must let go. That's the hard part, as many can't put it out into the air and then have the faith things will happen.*

✓ *Only worry about what you can control. Filling your brain with "what ifs" and possible negative scenarios will not only serve to be counter-productive, but it's also a waste of your precious time.*

✓ *Absorb what you learn during each step of the process.*

✓ *Ignore the naysayers. There is always going to be someone who doesn't understand or simply won't support you. Let that person be and get on with it.*

✓ *Embrace failure. Sometimes failing is a blessing. You can either learn from the error and fly higher on the next attempt or simply embark on another mission that is greater than you could ever have expected.*

Chapter 2

WOMEN VS. WOMEN

"If people like you, they're going to want to do business with you. And if they don't, you're going to have an almost insurmountable obstacle to overcome."

–Barbara Corcoran

When I was in high school, my best friend could have been my clone. Anyone who knew us would often say we may have been separated at birth. We shared common interests and similar personalities. We both sang and took vocal lessons from the same instructor. We both danced, and practiced ballet and jazz at the same dance school. We were both cheerleaders. We liked the same movies. We had the same taste in music. We loved the same foods. I could go on and on. She was (and still is) extraordinarily beautiful. Truly. From the inside out, Heather is the epitome of grace, femininity, sweetness, and light. She is a knockout. She stands about five foot six inches tall and has thick, gorgeous, long blonde hair, beautiful blue eyes, and a porcelain complexion. She was also always super smart. Heather and I were inseparable. Since our extracurricular activities were all in sync, spending time after school was easy. Although our classes were not always the same, our after-school curricular calendars were carbon copies of each other, so we were together five afternoons, every single week. On weekends, when not cheering or at play practice, we'd stroll the local mall, do lunch dates, and frequent TCBY, our very favorite indulgence. On most Saturday nights, we'd walk into parties together, after coordinating our fashion looks and having a glam session, and then we'd take turns sleeping over at each other's houses. For all four years of high school, that was our thing.

On more nights than I can count, Heather and I would artistically coordinate our outfits for the big Saturday night bash at the home of whichever classmate had parents out of town that weekend. Never would we toss on a simple t-shirt and jeans. Unfathomable. We would instead rock a sleek and well-fitted catsuit and accent belt, or a legging and sweater set, and if we did decide to dress down in jeans, they would be paired with a fabulous top full of glitz and glamour. Our hair was often coordinated too—usually down, hanging long on our backs, and our makeup was applied with precision. She and I were both models at our local mall and on their Teen Board, so we were much more savvy than typical teens regarding makeup technique. (Something that later came in handy for me when I started working in television news!)

Heather and I would strut into the party—always arriving late—and make a beeline for the spirit on hand. Never known to be too wild or too unruly, we were just the right amount of "cool" peppered in with a heaping dose of "good girl." She and I were both incredible students too. We were always on the honor roll, always chosen by school administrators for peer role model opportunities, and we each maintained close-knit and healthy relationships with our parents, siblings, and extended families. We were wholesome teenagers. Popular but not bad kids, well-rounded, and despite the fact that we were incredibly close, we both had our separate friend groups too. We had the perfect union. At school, because our maiden names both started with a "B," we often found ourselves seated near one another in homeroom, so that also meant our lockers were in close proximity. It all worked out perfectly. She was a best friend who was more like a sister, and I loved her. We helped each other through breakups, as well as navigating new boyfriends. We went to our proms together each year. Since we were really the only two in our vast friend groups who participated in the arts, our many friends would come to support us by attending our chorus concerts, cheering loudly at our dance recitals, and screaming our praise in the senior night talent show, when she and I did a singing duet and dance routine. It was a real hit and funny too: "Anything You Can Do, I Can Do Better." I still remember all the words and what we wore on stage! While Heather and I were both talented in our own right, it always seemed as though she had an upper hand. Despite how much I may have personally accomplished running a race in my own lane, her score card was always showing a higher number. Here's what I mean: We were both varsity cheerleaders, but Heather was also the squad captain. We were both talented ballet dancers, but Heather landed a solo in our final recital. We were both polished actresses, but Heather got the lead part in the school play, and so on. It honestly never bothered me, though. I looked up to her, and it always gave me something to work toward. She set the bar high, and I admired her for that.

Then, one day I realized our friendship, built on trust, mutual admiration, and love, also contained some hard-core, heated competition—more than I could ever imagine! I knew we were often vying for the same prize but never realized how hot the rivalry was becoming until I had a chance to compete in my county's preliminary pageant for Miss America. It was my mom's idea. She presented me with a newspaper clipping in the spring of my senior year of high school. Little did I know that I was about to embark on a life lesson no classroom would or could ever teach me. I had always loved watching the Miss America Pageant as a young girl, well into my then-late teen years. I would look forward to the pageant date each early September and was permitted to stay up late on those blissful Saturday nights until that year's winner was crowned. I remember most of those special nights were spent at my grandparents' home in Philadelphia. I keenly recall wearing a Miss Piggy felt night-gown while sitting on their plush navy-blue rug, a mere foot from their big-screen TV, with my eyes glued to the moni-tor. I had butterflies in my stomach and stars in my eyes. I was in awe. I was smitten by the glamour, glitz, talent, and the instant stardom these beautiful women all possessed.

They seemed like real-life princesses to me, and I admired them. I looked up to them and really, really wanted to be like them one day. My favorite portion of the competition was always the talent segment, but I really was entrenched in it all: the gowns, the commentating, the hosts' banter, the swimsuits; the women all seemed surreal to me. As I grew older, I would still watch the pageant with the same excitement and admiration but started to home in more so on the way the polished women took the stage, the way they answered questions posed by the judges, and how they sang, danced, played musical instruments, and showcased their talent. They seemed to really have it all. Intelligence, talent, poise, charm, and charisma. I had never had an opportunity to be in a pageant before, so when my mom found the casting call for "Miss Burlington County"—a preliminary pageant for Miss New Jersey and ultimately Miss America—I didn't hesitate for a second in giving her my answer: "YES!"

Selecting my talent was easy: I would sing, of course. Although I had various talents, singing was my strongest at that point. I had been studying voice for nearly six years, and loved, loved, loved to perform on stage. My platform was slightly more confusing to pick. At the age of eighteen, I was not worldly enough to have a deep appreciation for the hardships in our world. But I selected bullying awareness as my platform. Back then, it wasn't viewed as the epidemic that it is today but was just starting to be recognized for how detrimental it is. I had seen some bullying firsthand and did my part to defend the victim in a few different instances. I felt personally hurt by the nastiness I saw inflicted to a fellow student by this bully and the shame and humiliation the bully caused his victim to feel. It broke my heart, and I wanted to defend all victims of bullying and spread the word that this was a growing concern and should be recognized as a real danger to our youth.

As a future broadcast journalism student, I knew I would need to brush up on my current events for the interviewing process and that I might be dealt much more hard-hitting questions about politics and developing stories than some contestants might. But that didn't matter. I loved a good challenge and was always able to rise to the occasion. I would just study harder. I would push myself to learns the ins and outs of trending issues and topics and try my best to foresee what sorts of responses these judges may hope to evoke. No question, this part of the process was the most nerve-wracking. I never had a fear of public speaking, so standing at a podium in front of a panel of judges (most of whom were scowling) wasn't torturous for me. But the thought of undergoing live, rapid-fire questions about Iraq, the state of New Jersey politics, and the Rodney King police acquittal was nerve-wracking!

On the first day of rehearsals, we all gathered to introduce ourselves and begin the month-long prep work before the big competition. Contestants introduced themselves and spoke about their platforms, talents of choice, and interests; it seemed that most were already in college and had pageant experience. They were all new faces to me. All but one: Heather. It was a big surprise to see her among the other attractive and equally intelligent women. She had also signed up for the pageant and didn't tell me. Now, don't get me wrong, I was equally guilty of keeping the same secret.

At my mother's pleading, I did not tell Heather about my endeavor. My mom didn't mean ill will toward Heather. She just wanted me to participate in an activity without her by my side. Just once. I assumed that was also the reasoning Heather didn't share her involvement with me. We were both dumbfounded and embarrassed when we realized we had kept the same secret. At that instant, something shifted in our friendship. The trust was slightly chipped, and the sense of competition started to sink in. I know we both felt it.

Even still, we would take turns driving each Monday night to rehearsals at the Ramblewood County Club in Mount Laurel, New Jersey. We practiced walking, maneuvering our pivot turns, and speaking into the microphone to introduce ourselves to the live audience. We rehearsed our talent and the opening dance routine. It was a lot of fun, but I do remember (regretfully so) always sneaking a peak to see how Heather was doing, and I caught her doing the same to me. It was an unpleasant feeling. Envy. Jealousy. Competitiveness. There were thirteen contestants that year in the Miss Burlington County Pageant, but if you asked Heather or me how many we were competing against, our answer would likely have been one. Neither one of us walked away with the crown that year. But we both vowed we'd be back to compete again the following year. So, when our spring semester of college rolled around, she and I were both back in Burlington County, ready to hit the stage. We had lost touch a little bit, since we attended different universities. We still considered ourselves best friends, but there was no question that the rift that started at the pageant the year before was starting to gain new momentum. This time we meant business. I, for one, loved the whole pageant process and the friendships I made along the way. But truth be told, I really wanted the crown. So did she. We wanted it so we could go on and compete for Miss New Jersey. We wanted to get the precious scholarship money that went along with the title. We wanted the accolade on our resume. We wanted the local fame that would ensue. And we wanted to beat the other. It was a sad display.

Because we were both studying at colleges out of the area, we were excused from the month-long rehearsal prep. We were simply tasked with coming into town a few days before the pageant itself to swiftly learn the opening number and practice our talent on stage. No more carpooling, no more laughter and fun chats between practices. We had our eyes on the prize. I remember when the day of the final competition arrived, I was anxiously waiting to see what dress Heather had chosen for her evening gown competition. I was eager to see what swimsuit she'd be modeling and also what her talent costume looked like. I was interested in the others' too, and no doubt they were curious about my wardrobe selections, but Heather and I had tension between us. I hated it. It made me sad, and it felt uncomfortable.

Because each contestant is assigned a hostess or chaperone, it wasn't unusual that she and I were distracted with keeping pace and working hand-in-hand with the woman who was responsible for us. That kept us from feeling overly anxious about each other. We were distracted in a positive way. Having chaos around me and a laundry list of tasks to tackle on the pageant day leading up to that night's competition was a blessing. It forced me to focus on what I saw in the mirror, rather than on the sidelines. I didn't realize it then, but I was getting a real-life lesson about not looking at other women (especially your best friend!) as competition. Even if someone finishes ahead, and in pageants there is always just one winner, you can still simply compete with yourself. If you are more poised than the year before, perform stronger, and answer the judges' probes with more clarity and confidence, even if you don't win the title, you've won. That is a lesson I am often reminded of almost weekly as a professional businesswoman. No matter what ugliness comes my way, and trust me, I've seen a lot of gross displays from other women, I do not lower myself to their level. I always remind myself I'm only racing against me. I came out ahead that year. I placed as a runner up and was awarded some money for school, received a beautiful bouquet of roses, was pinned with a sash, and got lots of praise. It felt good, but looking back at Heather felt worse. The gain of the placement win was tremendous but not at the expense of the longstanding sisterhood we shared. I won my placement fair and square. I did not cheat, but I did shortchange myself in connection with my integrity. Heather matter-of-factly congratulated me, and I awkwardly said, "Thank you." I was proud of my accomplishment but ashamed of the competitive nature that I displayed. That was not the real me, and I vowed to myself I'd never utter such competitive self-talk to myself in that way again.

Later that year, one summer afternoon, while sunbathing at Heather's family pool, we had a real heart-to-heart and openly acknowledged our strained friendship. I don't remember who started the conversation, but once we broached the subject, we didn't hold back. Crying, we spoke about how our friendship had warped and how we wanted things between us to be the way it had once been. We went on to update each other very honestly about our boyfriends. We were both in relationships, but neither of us was fully content. I offered Heather advice about her situation, and she shared some insight and suggestions regarding my own circumstance. We then went on to discuss what was going on at our campuses. I had just decided I was not going to continue cheering at Hofstra. It was a hard decision to make, given how competitive it had been to make the team in the first place, but I wanted to explore other interests pertaining to my major and I wanted to pledge a sorority. Heather, who had pledged her sorority in the fall of her freshman year, shared what it was like to be an active sister and live in a sorority house. We also confessed our worries regarding our classes and career plans. I was on a fast track to be a news reporter, and while Heather was a decided double major of international business and Spanish studies, she wasn't exactly sure what her first "real" job would look like. It was one of the most honest and deep conversations that she and I had had since high school. I felt peace. I felt at home. We laughed, we cried, and we hugged very tightly that afternoon. Without any deep discussion about how things unraveled at the pageant, we stayed focused on our bond and how we deeply missed one another. That was a turning point. We agreed that no prize, not even a pageant crown, was worth battling over. We'd work to our own best potential and let the chips fall where they may. We both shared how we wanted to give it another shot at the pageant the following spring, but promised we'd stay focused on ourselves and cheer on the other in tandem. That practice came in handy for me throughout my career. I may not have been vying against my best friend for a promotion or account, but in many cases, I've been subconsciously betting against women I care about and/or respect. I've learned to do so with grace and with dignity. Even if the other party doesn't share that mindset.

Two years ago, I launched my first book. I was beyond blessed to attain a publisher, which gives an author a great deal of credibility on so many levels that I believe self-publishing simply cannot. There was a fellow author who also launched a book around the same time. While this woman was not in my line of work nor did she share similar interests or friends with me, for a variety of reasons she was competitive with me. Although we weren't in contact during the book launches, I was made aware that she had an unhealthy interest in my book. She wanted to know how many people showed up at my book signings, how my book sales were going, how much press I was securing versus what she was getting. Around the same time, I unfortunately was the victim of some ugly and ill-willed book reviews, which seemed exceptionally questionable because the reviewers didn't have much to say about the book's content. Instead, the review platform was used to attack me personally. At first, I was angry, more than hurt, and wanted revenge. I was sure this woman was to blame. Many in my court suggested that I act similarly and post negative reviews about her book so that she'd feel the same backlash. But I didn't do that. I also chose to believe (after a lot of soul searching) that the disturbing reviews were not written by her. I'm still not sold on that theory, but I choose to tell myself that story rather than the uglier one, so that I am able to rise above the situation.

About six months after the negative review ordeal, our paths crossed, and I chose, again, to take the road of kindness. An influential colleague of mine had asked me to sit on a panel of female authors for an event in Philadelphia. The gathering was to be attended by other influential who's who in the city, and in addition to public speaking (which I believe is my calling and I have made a second career out of it) I was going to be able to sign and sell books after the panel discussion concluded. I was later informed by the event coordinators that one of the six scheduled authors had to cancel due to an emergency, and they asked me if I could recommend another author to join in her place. I pondered the situation and then decided to reach out to this woman to see if she would be interested. I was trying to help my colleague but more so trying to help her as a fellow author, despite the fact she had never helped me. I felt it was the kind thing to do. If her book did well, great for her. If my book did well, great for me. If someone bought her book, that didn't mean someone else wouldn't buy my book. If she got recognition, it didn't take any sunlight off of my face. In the end, the woman declined, and that was just fine. I did the right thing, and that's all that mattered. That's my mantra. Kindness always. Always be kind. Even when they're not.

Heather and I went on to compete our final two years of college but never won, which was okay. We already had a prize in each other. The Miss Burlington County Pageant gave me so much more than a crown. It brought much anxiety and lots of emotions, but most of all it gave me a foundation for something so much more: the game of life. Through trial and error, mistakes and milestones, I truly evolved into a poised, well-spoken, confident, and untattered version of myself. The pageant process was incredibly fun. Once a year, for one weekend, I got a small sampling of what stardom could feel like. The pageant was glamorous, and I did learn beauty tricks and techniques I still use today. But the pageant organization truly gifted me so much more than that.

During the grilling interview process, I learned to stand on my own in the heat of the fire and how to handle tough questions without showing I was melting inside. And, even if I didn't know all the answers to the judges' probes, I learned how to respond in the best way I could with confidence and grace. I also learned to speak up, smile when what I really wanted to do was cry, and to push my shoulders back instead of crumble at the seams. I learned what losing (in front of a live audience) felt like, as well as winning. I learned, too, how winning can make you feel uncomfortable and awkwardly guilty, as I felt when looking back at Heather the year I placed. I learned how to be humble and to praise my fellow contestants. How not to look at others as competition and to run my own race with my eyes fixed on my lane. I also learned to take criticism in stride. How one's opinion is truly subjective and what someone might hate or love could be completely opposite from another. That lesson came in especially handy when I later entered the cutthroat and often callous TV news industry, an overly critical and often hurtful field.

But the biggest gift the pageant gave me—beyond the scholarship, beyond the amazing friendships I still maintain, and even beyond those cherished moments on stage when I sang my heart out—the pageant gifted me, me. A confident, classy, delicate-yet-strong me. I would not have had a successful television news career, be the entrepreneur I am today, have the courage to believe in myself enough to follow my heart and leave a ten-year marriage, or pour my heart and soul into a memoir without my pageant experience.

Pageants are not for everyone. They get a bad rap, sometimes for a good reason, and that makes me sad. They have their place. Just like it's awesome to be a jock or flaunt forms of masculinity (which is especially applauded and rightfully so) it's also more than okay to be feminine, to be dainty and polished and poised like a princess. I am a princess, but not the stereotypical kind you see in a Disney movie. I'm feminine and fierce, and I have the Miss America Organization to thank for that.

Don't Be a Bitch Bullets #2

Supporting Your Sisters

✓ *Form a close circle of female friends who are like-minded or in similar industries or maintain comparable titles.*

✓ *Amplify your female coworker's hard work, recent achievement, or contribution. Brag about her to teammates or your boss. Boost her up, and others will be inspired to take positive actions too.*

✓ *Build a bond outside of the office. It's equally important that you maintain strong ties with female coworkers on a personal level, in addition to a professional one.*

✓ *Show up for your sisters on social media. Retweet her comments, share her Instagram stories, and compliment her on her posts. That support will go a long way.*

✓ *Take the time to be a mentor in some shape or form. We can all learn from one another, regardless of rank.*

Chapter 3

THE MYTH OF THE BITCH

"When we surround ourselves with negative or toxic people, we often start to mirror their negativity."

–Jamie Kern Lima, multimillionaire
founder of IT Cosmetics

Many female entrepreneurs believe that they will get further with salt than with sugar. I couldn't disagree with them more. True, you never want your team to see you melt and you need to maintain an aura of strength, but more often than not, when it comes to female leaders, so many equate strength to being an outright bitch. We have the onslaught of those once-trendy "bitch books" to thank for that mentality. They claim that harnessing a "bitch boss" attitude is the only way to climb the ladder and reach the top. They think that a "Don't mess with me or else," mindset is key to getting ahead and staying relevant. Wrong. I don't believe women need to pretend to be tough and mean in order to get ahead. The mindset of a bitch boss is to run a business as if she were being constantly attacked. Always on the defense. Ready to go to war. You don't need to be a full-scale warrior to be a winner. You just need to exude confidence—earned confidence, through trial and error—which, after all, is the real warpath in business.

Many women also mistakenly feel that to be seen and heard in the workplace, they need to be feared. After all, we've all been told, "Nice girls don't get the corner office," at some point in our careers. We've also been told to tone down the girly persona, behave more like a man, and toughen our skin. True, to some degree, thick skin is a necessary tool to carry in one's briefcase, but it never should double as a weapon. In a *Forbes* article entitled, "The Bitching Point," Meghan Casserly explores how women are expected to hold their own in a sea of men, but their assertiveness often is interpreted as aggression. I've seen in my own life how that can be perceived negatively.

When I worked in television news, I had the privilege of working for and with some of the greatest leaders in local broadcast news. They all had their unique management styles and one thing in common: the news directors were all men. Most of their direct reports were male too. At the NBC affiliate I anchored for in Louisiana, the executive producer was a guy. At NBC in Champaign, Illinois, the second in command was a man. In New Castle, Delaware, same drill. And the list goes on and on. They were all well respected, extremely talented, and hardworking. I admired them very much but learned early on that the higher you climb in business, the less even the playing field really is. Truth be told, less than 5 percent of Fortune 500 CEOs are female, according to the Center for American Progress. Despite the fact that women earn more than half of all undergraduate and master's degrees, they still lag when it comes to assuming leadership roles in corporate America. At law firms, 45 percent of associates are women but less than 25 percent are partners. In medicine, women make up 40 percent of doctors and surgeons but only 16 percent are permanent medical school deans. And in finance, 61 percent of all accountants and auditors are women but less than 13 percent are financial officers at Fortune 500 companies. So, to stand up against gender discrimination, many women feel the need to double down and get mean with the men (and women) in the boardroom.

I've encountered my fair share of bitches, even after my bout working for QB. Women in media, women who run businesses my firm has collaborated with, and women who were clients. Luckily for me, I can pick and choose who I do business with, but in some cases, the bitch factor didn't present itself until later on after a relationship had already been established. One such client comes to mind. This high-end salon and spa consisted of not one but four female owners who all brought different talents to the proverbial table. One partner was the executive director; another led the creative side of the hair division; another ran the skincare and aesthetics departments; and the fourth was in charge of marketing. She was the partner I worked most with. She was also the partner I liked the least. Although the women all presented themselves as collaborative with one another and team players upon hiring my firm to help with their public relations initiatives, they were anything but when push came to shove. Needless cattiness, constant and unnecessary drama, and evident backstabbing were always erupting. I often felt as though I was caught in the middle of the chaos as each partner needed to flex her muscles to the others and to the team of one hundred plus stylists and assistants. It was an utter nightmare.

I often felt myself explaining to my team back at the MB offices how we needed to "rise above" the pandemonium and simply do our job. More times than I can count, media opportunities were put at risk due to the lack of cooperation on the part of the female partners. Clearly, they just couldn't see the benefit of letting one lead at a time. Instead of relinquishing power to each other, they would butt heads and stand in one another's way just to be seen and heard. I finally had to put my foot down and step away after one crazy incident occurred involving the local Fox station in Philadelphia and a lack of cooperation on their part to get the segment properly executed and on the air.

It was early fall in 2014, and my team and I were actively researching what the new and trending hairstyles were for the upcoming winter season. Each season, in addition to the media outreach efforts to promote projects, new services, or treatments inside the salon and spa, we would research which beauty trends celebrities were dabbling with and what the high-end fashion and beauty magazines were covering to see how this particular salon and spa could tap that. The clients expect this regular due diligence. We never rely on the client to come up with content. If they can add to our campaign plan, it's just an added bonus. We gathered some ideas to present to the owners for approval, and one trend was very evident: the idea of recreating hair color hues to match that of your favorite Starbucks coffee drinks. For instance, an auburn shade of hair adorned with some caramel-colored highlights might be coined, "The Pumpkin Spice," and a lighter shade perhaps, "The Blondie," and so on. It was an adorable spin for winter hair color in a season in which not much was happening. All the buzz was around it, and the media was eating it up (figuratively and literally). I knew it would be a homerun among the local press too.

Each month, we would meet the four partners for a recap meeting where we'd discuss current media outreach, what was booked on the calendar, and forecast new ideas. At this meeting, however, one of the partners was absent. She was away on a weekend trip with her family and had left the other three to proceed. Totally not a big deal at all. In addition, as this partner typically handled more of the back-of-the-business tasks, it was not necessary that she even be in attendance. As we presented the three women with our new winter ideas we wanted to begin pitching in the coming week, the coffee hair color was top on our list. Everyone raved. They loved it. It would breathe new life into their hair color department, which on its own had few new developments to share. No new highlighting techniques, no new hair color products, and no new hot "must-try" color for the winter of 2015. It was an otherwise very boring hair color season. Incidentally, the hair color department is the biggest money maker in most salons. The price ticket is usually high, and it's a service most need to have on repeat. Frequently. Anything to boost a salon's color department is always welcome. The coffee color trend was a go. And, so, we were on it like white on rice, pitching the trend to beauty writers in Philadelphia and southern New Jersey. The plan was that one of the salon's expert colorists would speak to the trend and how to achieve it, as well as offer tips regarding which coffee shades complimented which skin tones best. We'd showcase three models to illustrate before and after looks (before the color treatment and after) so that the viewing audience would get a clear picture of what the shades looked like on real people. When we pitched the idea to the Fox station, the producers jumped on it for their "Good Day, Philadelphia!" segment, which was the perfect platform for a light-hearted, fun, and informative beauty segment. Perfect!

The producers wanted the segment to be done live, which meant that the models needed their hair colored in advance. Only the "reveal" would be shown on TV in real time. That scenario was much easier to execute because "before" images could be taken during the lengthy coloring process and flashed during the colorist's interview portion before the actual "reveal." This was the most simple way to pull it off and also showcase the salon. There was one glitch, though. The fourth owner, the woman who was away on a weekend getaway when we discussed the idea in our latest campaign meeting, didn't like the correlation to coffee and instead wanted to call the hair color shades what they technically were, "auburn with caramel highlights," or "two-tone blonde highlights on light brown hair." It was a nightmare! That pulled the segment back into boring and dull arena and was not what I had pitched the producer. There was no way the news team would agree to proceed with this segment unless we stuck to the original plan.

I was really in a spot. I had worked so hard to "sell" this story to the news producer, and my client was giving me pushback. Because I had never tossed a client under the proverbial bus, I would have to take the fall for why this segment never happened if we had to cancel. That sort of scenario is most unfavorable and often results in a producer choosing to ignore future story ideas—the kiss of death to a publicist. In a last-ditch effort to salvage the segment and maintain camaraderie with the producing team, I took an in-person meeting with this testy partner (AKA the bitch in this story) to hear her out and explain why calling a color shade a coffee hue is a good idea. As we sat in her cramped salon office and she sifted through emails while glancing in my direction, it was obvious she didn't care what I had to say. The mere fact that she was not a part of the decision-making process that led to the positive result of a strong media opportunity was clearly on the top of her mind. Forget the 4.1 million viewers who may see the segment and would want to try the color trend out for themselves, or at the very least think of the salon as the region's premier beauty destination, given their prominent feature on this morning news program. She wasn't budging. She wanted to show her weight, and I could tell her issue had nothing to do with the segment itself but with her partners. My hunch was that she wasn't being heard. I suspected that she felt as though her voice was not being respected internally, so in an effort to prove her worth in the company, she was sabotaging this opportunity. She needed to prove a point, and the only way she knew how was to be a bitch. She succeeded.

The segment fell apart, and even though I apologized profusely to the news producer, she was understandably angry and disappointed. When I sold my story idea to her initially, she then had to sell it to her boss. Now she had to go back and explain why it wasn't going to happen. Really bad. All the way around. In time (and thankfully not a very long time) the ordeal of the canceled segment was forgotten. But I was reminded of what a bitch boss looks like soon thereafter. Each of the partners took a turn in the bitch seat almost on rotation. They weren't necessarily bitchy to me but to one another. It was mind-boggling. As they all struggled with power, voice, and relevance, it appeared that the only card they knew how to play well was the bitch one. Instead of speaking in a calm, cool, and collected tone or listening to each other and trying to make fair and impartial decisions, they bickered one after the other. Each tried to out-bitch the other as if it were the only tactic she had. How sad. Eventually, I got sick of it. My team did too. It was a very immature and unproductive way to do business. Showing your worth and having your voice heard over the noise isn't always easy. Some days I feel it's frankly exhausting, but having a sense of calm, a sense of care, and a sense of class will far outweigh a bitchy and nasty course of communication time and time again. I'd rather dismiss myself from a disagreement and revisit at a later time before I would ever lower myself to bitch mode.

You don't need to be a bitch to be a boss. You need to exude confidence, empathy, and assertiveness. But you don't need to be a bitch. None of those qualities equate to "bitch-dom," but are, rather, the epitome of a smart, sophisticated, and confident woman. Facebook COO Sheryl Sandberg is famous for highlighting how bossy women are more likely to face consistent pushback and eventually lose out on promotions. Her notion has been proven too, with various studies and surveys. She even started a campaign to ban the word bossy, and instead encourage women to stand up for themselves and not be afraid of being assertive. I'm with her on that. You can be assertive, but you don't need to be a bitch to do it.

Be Bold Without Being a Bitch

✓ *Stay authentic. Be your true self. There's a fine line between being aggressive and being arrogant. If you stay true to your core self, you'll steer clear of negative territory.*

✓ *Make a move. Taking the first step toward a project or a solution is applaudable. Then, seek out allies to help you finish the feat.*

✓ *Don't waste energy on unsupportive colleagues. Fighting an uphill battle just to prove a point isn't always the productive path to take. Focus on the frontline and steer clear of negativity.*

✓ *Welcome disagreement. You can be passionate about your beliefs and still listen to those with differing points of view. Disagreement is necessary for smart decision-making.*

✓ *Create a revolution, not a rebellion. Rebellions are synonymous with fault and blame while revolutions inspire people to come together and create newness.*

Chapter 4

MEMORABLE MENTORS

"If you are successful, it is because somewhere,
sometime, someone gave you a life or an idea
that started you in the right direction."

–Melinda Gates

The greatest gift you can be granted as an up-and-coming professional is an amazing mentor. I have been incredibly blessed to have a plethora of exceptional mentors throughout my career. At every stage of my professional life, I've had the extreme good fortune to have had those who have traveled the road before me, shared their experiences, and taken the time and care to mold me, shape me, and, when necessary, reprimand me so that I could evolve into the best professional version of myself. Even today, after spending ten years as a television news anchor and reporter, and now CEO of MB and Associates for almost two decades, I still seek out mentors. I am always eager and excited to connect with other public relations professionals, both older and younger, to learn from. The older and seasoned talent share their legacy of knowledge and achievements while the younger and sometimes wiser talent share their proficiency in technology, conquering social media, and knowing much more than I about today's tricks in video shooting and editing. In many ways, I lean on the younger talent just as they lean on me to guide and nurture them. A mentor doesn't have to be older than you or have been in the workforce longer. A mentor is simply anyone who is generous with their time and their mind and has something to offer you so that you can grow and expand. In business, even more so than monetary rewards, I believe a mentor is the most coveted gift we can be given.

As Benjamin Franklin famously said, "Tell me and I forget, teach me and I may remember, involve me and I learn." It's so true! When you lean on a mentor, you're tapping into a wealth of knowledge that can accelerate your learning curve by incredible measures. When I was a sophomore in college, I secured an internship opportunity at the ABC station in Philadelphia, months before the assistant news director even began his search for summer intern candidates. That was always my style. Always early to the playing field, always eager, and always aggressive. Because I had reached out to him many months before the pool of potential interns for the summer session, he allowed me to pick my shift. I had the option of the dayside shift, which meant coming in at standard hour of 9 a.m. and working until 6 p.m., or I could take the lone morning intern spot, which started at 4 a.m. and wrapped up at 1 p.m. Early morning hours in television are commonplace and eventually wound up being my norm throughout my television news career, but for a college student, starting the day at 4 a.m. (which meant rising at 2:30 a.m. to shower and drive thirty minutes to the station each morning) sounded torturous. I'm not going to lie; it still sort of does! But he then went on to share that the dayside shift entailed working at the assignment desk. He also said I would be one of four or five interns and likely not have as much hands-on experience as the morning intern would. If I could handle the early hours, he shared I'd get to work hand-in-hand with the show's producers and also likely get to assist the anchors and reporters. That's all I needed to hear. I was sold. "I want the morning shift, please!" I immediately announced. I'd just go back to the bedtime routine I maintained when I was in kindergarten for that summer! I didn't care. I wanted to learn and grow. I had no idea how much I would distend that summer.

In 1994, the morning news at 6ABC was on the air at 5 a.m. (Now they are on the air even earlier!) Highest in ratings in that market, the show was co-anchored by Monica Malpass and Rick Williams. That was the channel my parents would always have the TV turned to, and both anchors were famous. I was beyond exhilarated to be working in the same room as them! The morning producer and the noon producer were so talented, so smart, and so willing to let me ask questions and offer my services beyond what was expected of me. I also befriended an editor who would let me retrack (reproduce) stories other reporters had done, so that I could get experience doing a voiceover, working on a stand-up (appearing on camera for a part of the story), and more. But I think my real reporter skills blossomed that summer by watching and working with Rick. Rick was a no-nonsense newsman, and I respected him tremendously. It wasn't a part of my daily duties, but when I was finished supporting the morning show and waiting for the scripts to be written and printed for the noon show, I would walk over to Rick's desk in the back of the newsroom and see if he had any work he could pass to me. He often did, and I was thrilled! Sometimes, he'd have me do some research for a story he was interested in or preliminary interviews so that he could gather facts needed to determine if the story was worth covering. He looked at my standups and offered me constructive criticism. He also gave me writing tips, which helped me hone my style. But most of all, what I cherished the most from serving as an intern under Rick was his stories. He shared stories of working in much smaller markets (the station size I was likely to land in post-graduation). He shared what it was like just starting out in the business, about his college life, and what his internships were like. He shared how hard he worked and gave me real insight into the television news business. Those conversations were invaluable.

I had the pleasure of sitting down with Rick to reminisce about my internship at his station in preparation for writing this book. Rick is now the 5 p.m. and 10 p.m. anchor at 6ABC and has been employed there for now more than thirty years, the second longest standing employee at the station! He's a household name, now more than ever, but still the same polished, humble, and warm-hearted soul he was twenty-six years ago. "What I remember most about you, Mindie," he shared with me via a Zoom interview, "was that you were always asking questions. You were always eager to learn, and you did more than what was expected of you." I was touched by his kind words and recollection. But what he may not realize is that because he was so open with me, he enabled me to be the best asset to 6ABC I possibly could. Had he been unapproachable or unkind, I would never have had the courage as a twenty-year-old to walk up to his fancy desk, in the back of a quiet newsroom where all the 6ABC stars sat, and interrupt him, asking for an assignment. I was a great intern because he was a great mentor. No question! Rick and I are still extremely close. I still look to him for advice and guidance, since my role now as a publicist is so intricately entwined with the news business. He and his wife have become very dear friends. We often meet for dinners out in the city. We've done outings with my children, and I consider both more like family. That's the power of being a positive role model!

Film phenom George Lucas once shared, "Mentors have a way of seeing more of our faults than we would like. It's the only way we grow." A good mentor will be brutally honest with you and tell you exactly how it is, rather than sugarcoating to spare your feelings. Allison Gibson did that for me. When I was midway into my television news career, I was a reporter at News 12 New Jersey. The station was aired and owned by Cablevision at the time and was a real powerhouse. I gained such incredible experience working at that station. I nailed my first live shot there. I served for a time as the station's political reporter, working out of a bureau in the New Jersey State House and across the hall from the governor. I covered the 9/11 terrorist attack at the World Trade Center and its aftermath. My experience at News 12 New Jersey helped make me a solid and stellar reporter, but Allison gave me my wings.

She was the assistant news director at the time and very hands-on. She led our daily morning meeting with reporters, photographers, and assignment editors. She would listen intently as we all pitched story ideas for that day's coverage. If she didn't like your idea or it was apparent you didn't do your homework to prepare, she called you out on it. She wasn't mean and she didn't lash out, but she was stern and firm, and we all took her very seriously. In fact, on my second day working at the station, I was so worried about making a good impression that I made a terrible mistake. I was really sick. I didn't have a fever and was told by my doctor that I was not contagious, but I should have called out for the day. I had a sinus infection and wasn't feeling well at all. But it was my second day on the job, and I was worried that it would appear I was slacking off. I was taking an antibiotic for the illness, and for whatever reason, I chose not to eat breakfast before I left for work. Prepared for the morning meeting, armed with a decent amount of story ideas, I walked into the news director's glass corner office feeling confident. The office was big but lacked seating for everyone. Normally, this would not be a big deal. The meeting was usually only fifteen to thirty minutes and we would just stand around and wait for our turn to share ideas. Then, Allison would make the dayside assignments. But as I stood there waiting to speak, I started feeling nauseous. Was I just nervous to share my ideas? I'll admit I was intimidated and always worried what Allison would think of my pitches. But I didn't think that was what was causing my stomach to churn. Then, it was my turn to speak. I shared my ideas. She liked them! Sigh. But the queasiness didn't dissipate after I went to bat. It got worse! Now, my head was spinning, and I felt my heart racing. I was also breaking out into a clammy sweat. I desperately wanted to sit down, but that would have entailed sitting on the floor. I was in a skirt suit and knew that I'd look ridiculous as well as draw attention to myself. That wasn't going to happen! Instead, I prayed the meeting would end soon so I could go find a chair at the closest desk and collapse into it. I needed to just get off my feet, get myself centered, and catch my breath. But as soon as the meeting concluded, the assignment editor called me over to share the sources he had for my assigned story. So, I couldn't sit down! Instead, I stood by the big, impressive assignment desk, smack in the middle of the newsroom and situated on a mini stage of sorts. As he was rattling off the information he had for me, I interrupted him. "I don't feel so…" was all I could get out until I blacked out, right in the middle of the newsroom, nearly falling face-first onto the floor! Thankfully, he caught me as I fainted and saved my head from hitting the carpet. I gained consciousness a few seconds later to look up to a crowd of very concerned new colleagues. If they didn't know me before, they certainly knew me now! OMG! Allison was among them, and she was equally worried and helped a few male photographers carry me into a nearby conference room to rest. I wanted to die! Now I was causing the station stress and extra work! They brought me some juice and crackers and asked me many questions about what I had eaten, was I sick, etc. I shared the fact that I had a sinus infection and was taking an antibiotic. They called the paramedics and when they took my vital signs and the medical professionals ran their own line of questioning, they confirmed that the fainting spell was likely caused by the combination of taking an antibiotic and not eating. They advised that I see my regular doctor that day and that I not drive home. So, Allison pulled two photographers off their assignment to help. One to drive me home in their news vehicle and the other to drive my personal car from Edison, NJ back to Cherry Hill, where I was living, a full ninety minutes away! All I cared about was the aggravation I was causing. I knew that taking two photographers out of work to drive three hours round-trip would mean they couldn't shoot news that day. What a strain for the station! I had another solution: I could stay and help the producer with writing for the day, and then they could take me back after their assignments had been shot. Allison laughed. She must have thought I was insane. She insisted this was all fine and that the news coverage would also be strong that night, despite this setback. She also understood why I hadn't called out sick. She was so incredible to me that day. She didn't make me feel bad. Instead, she empowered me and made me feel welcomed despite the annoyance I know I must have caused that morning.

She was all this and more to me during my tenure at News 12. Another intimidating daily encounter I went through there was script approval. Just before a reporter would track and edit their story, they would send their written script to Allison for review. She read each script before it made air and would often redline items she thought needed more facts, detail, or simply needed to be cut. Every script approval meeting meant changes, and I loved it. I was, however, always mildly frightened to hear what she would say. Not because she was mean but because I cared so much about what she thought. All I wanted was to please her. I respected her; I looked up to her; I worshipped her professional opinion as my boss and as my mentor. What she had to say meant everything to me. Each meeting, she would share her critique, but in a way where I would walk away with a lesson, not a smackdown. She would explain why she thought the story could be better with more of this or that and helped me tremendously with my writing. I also recently had the pleasure of sitting down with Allison, who is now a news director in Iowa, to learn about what her thoughts were of having me as a mentee. She shared that she always looked forward to our encounters and that she valued not only my talent and professionalism but the upbeat energy and enthusiasm I brought into the entire newsroom. "You were always a ray of sunshine," Allison shared on a call a few months ago. "I'm sorry I never shared that with you back then." I can't express how much those words meant to me. Even today, I cherish Allison, as my mentor, my friend, and someone who has made a positive and powerful impact on my career. I am a better boss, a better mentor, and a much better writer because of her!

As Oprah Winfrey once said, "A mentor is someone who allows you to see the hope inside yourself." Mentors are there no matter what and will offer you uplifting advice when the going gets tough. They're also sounding boards we can bounce ideas off of to obtain an unedited response. A mentor is a trusted advisor. In the business world, it's not always easy to determine who is trustworthy and who is only pretending to be your ally. This notion becomes especially profound when spilling proprietary information to another. Janet Zappala is all that and more to me. I never interned for Janet, nor did I ever "work" for her, but I was lucky enough to have worked with Janet not once but twice during my time in television news. Earlier in my career, I served as a writer and segment producer at the Fox station in Philadelphia, where she was a reporter and anchor. We first bonded at that station, as I would pass her in the newsroom or in the ladies' room, where we would make small talk. I instantly liked her. Like Rick, Janet was someone I watched on television before I worked in the field. I was always impressed with her talent, but when I got to know her personally, she won my heart. She was (and still is) warm, hardworking, incredibly upbeat, and eager to offer me advice and encouragement whenever she can. A few jobs later, we found ourselves sharing a newsroom again, this time at TSM News, which eventually became part of the Comcast Network. There, we were more laterally aligned, as I was the morning anchor and she was the nightside anchor. She had a bigger role than I had, but we sat at the same anchor desk. I felt like I was dreaming! At that point in my career, I still had much to learn (I still do—we never stop learning!), and Janet was more than happy to help me whenever she could. We would get together at her home in suburban Philadelphia, and she would watch my anchor reels and assess my performance, my delivery, and more.

She would offer critiques and sound advice I could implement in the next show. She also offered me insurmountable career climbing advice. She shared details about her own journey, how she started in news working at a station in Bakersfield, California, followed by a stint in Hawaii and later in Denver, before landing in Philadelphia. She gave me her personal insight too. At the time, Janet was married to her second husband and spoke to me about what life was like as a working mom, as well as when she made the difficult decision to leave her first husband in pursuit of her career. With wide eyes and open ears, I soaked it all up. I took each word she spoke to heart and loved every single second of those afternoons with Janet!

She and I remain close to this day. Now an author herself and a nutritionist, she taps me as needed to support her with publicity for her amazing projects. She also supports me in immeasurable ways. When I was on tour promoting *Intermission*, she attended one of my West Coast book signings, and afterward we enjoyed a fun dinner, full of laughs and lots of love. Janet has been on my podcast, "The Race for the Ring," and I've made appearances on her Instagram Live series. Janet is a lifelong friend. She's my "sister from another mister," as we possess the same high-energy and "can-do" attitude. I adore Janet in more ways than words could ever express. She didn't pay my salary, like a boss would have, but she's filled me with more riches than any paycheck ever has!

Don't Be a Bitch Bullets #4

Soak Up the Sun

✓ *Be clear about your "ask." Mentees who grow the most are those who are clearest on what they want and ask for it. Mentees should be honest about what they want and ask for it.*

✓ *Be courageous. The most successful mentees ask the most questions, even when the answers seem obvious. Don't be afraid to raise your hand, inquire, and relish the information shared.*

✓ *All feedback is a gift. Even when the words shared may sting, you need to look at all constructive criticism as an opportunity to grow and evolve from another who's "been there, done that."*

✓ *Be prepared. Always come with a plan of attack, a vision to execute, or a potential solution to a problem.*

✓ *Show gratitude. Always. Mentors are sharing their time, wisdom, and valuable experience. A good mentee will provide feedback and be gracious for the experience and impact the relationship has had on their life.*

Chapter 5

NURTURING THE NEWBIES

*"Don't just kick open doors. Hold them open
and invite others to step through."*

–Jo Miller, female leadership expert

In nearly twenty years, MB and Associates has hired forty-plus interns and young associates over the years, most of whom were women. As I approach my eighteenth anniversary of being in business, I am proud to have had a role in helping launch many into fabulous careers. Many of them I keep in touch with. One specializes in literary public relations and works for a firm that represents some of the nation's hottest authors. One former employee is now employed in the marketing and public relations division for Comcast, the Philadelphia-based cable giant, and another has opened a boutique firm that is based in Denver, Colorado. Their success warms my heart. And then there's Jenna Stark, a marketing and advertising superstar who got her start with MB and Associates as a high school student and returned in her sophomore year of college. A two-time intern. Jenna is devoted, allegiant, and one of the young talents I take the most pride in seeing soar.

Jenna was only sixteen when we met back then, and I took her under my wing. At the time, a ritzy boutique in suburban New Jersey had hired me to create a monthly "Girls Night Out" event for its upscale designer-clad clientele. (You will read more about this event in Chapter 8!) Everyone involved was much older than she was, but she did a superior job assisting me. I was sorry to see her go, but we stayed in touch. Later, as a student at the University of Delaware, she returned to MB to intern with me in exchange for college credit. I was thrilled to have her back! She was so reliable and hardworking that it felt like she was an actual employee instead of a college student just there for her summer break. I remember spending a lot of time with Jenna, listening to her ideas and teaching her everything I could about the ins and outs of the public relations business. Has it ever paid off!

Today, she is the Director of Partnerships and Strategy at Katie Couric Media—yes *that* Katie Couric. Katie and her husband, John Molner (CEO), started their multiplatform media company in 2017. Jenna works closely with the leadership team at KCM to help create content that sparks curiosity, elevates the conversation, and most importantly inspires action to move the world forward. She forges partnerships that build KCM's awareness and audience, while also working with the top brands in the world as they collaborate with KCM to create their own purpose-driven content that will connect with millions of consumers.

Before joining KCM, Jenna worked with another media powerhouse, British-born media mogul Tina Brown, the former editor of *Vanity Fair* and the author of *The Diana Chronicles*. In 2009, Tina created "Women in the World," a live journalism platform designed to uplift female voices around the globe. Jenna's job was to put together sponsorship deals for the annual events, which have featured Oprah Winfrey, Hillary Clinton, and Anna Wintour, among others. Jenna also is a former national advertising director for *New York Magazine*, which chronicles life, culture, politics, and style in Manhattan. You could say that when Jenna lands on her feet, she has a fabulous pair of Jimmy Choos just waiting for her feet to slide into. Just thinking of her momentum and no-nonsense attitude makes me smile!

Over the years, Jenna and I have become incredibly close friends, as well as business associates, since our early days of working together. We share confidences about our career journeys and bounce things off each other about what we are going through. Our relationship has gotten to the point that I lean on her just as much as she leans on me—sometimes more. A few years ago, I was experiencing some serious financial challenges with MB and Associates while I was launching my first book, and I didn't have the bandwidth to handle a book tour, run a business, and work on cultivating business development. I was under a lot of pressure racing from city to city, appearing on TV programs, and working late nights and weekends appearing at book signings. In addition, I still had the normal workload at MB and Associates. But I had been so focused on the book tour that I hadn't been bringing in new clients like I usually do, and it felt like my entire world was about to come crashing down on me. When you're a sole proprietor like I am, you don't always have someone to talk to or get advice from. I could have reached out to some of my girlfriends, but that did not feel right. They have their own lives and concerns and do not always have the time or the patience to listen to me discuss the intricacies of my business. So, I reached out to the one person who I knew would understand my debacle and could relate to what I was going through: Jenna! She and I arranged to meet for a late lunch at our go-to spot in New York, the Loews Regency Hotel's Regency Bar & Grill on Park Avenue. I was already in the area, since it is near the headquarters of the Julien Farel Restore Salon & Spa. The Regency is an upscale, see-and-be-seen kind of place. Normally, I would have enjoyed checking out the crowd to see who was there and soaking up the sumptuous ambiance. But on that particular day, all I could think about was how bad things were for MB and Associates. Over cocktails, I told Jenna about what I was going through and how I had gotten to this point. I'll have to say that she listened intently before jumping in and saying, "You've got to cut the fat! You are going to have to lay off people. You have to cut their hours. You have to just, like, cut, cut, cut!" I was not used to that, since business has been so good for us, each and every year. It was unusual to hear another perspective. She really helped me strategize about what to do. We literally put our heads together over that white tablecloth-covered banquette and came up with a drastic, cost-saving plan: I would get rid of my expensive New York City apartment, put my furniture in storage, and commute to and from Jersey for six months. She even offered to let me sleep on her couch if I needed a place to stay, which was so kind of her. I would trim unnecessary business expenses and hold off on hiring an associate to replace another who had resigned a few months prior. Luckily, it never came to that, since our business rebounded, and swiftly. Still, it was awesome to have someone to talk things out with. I will forever be grateful for my friendship with Jenna. I honestly consider Jenna family and one of my closest friends. But the reality is that we would not have the amazing relationship that we do today had I not invested all I did into her all of those years ago and she into her role in my company. I am glad that I really took the time to help her grow and learn and get a toehold in public relations.

I make a point of trying to do the same thing with my other interns and young talent. I have never forgotten that I was an intern once myself who needed direction and instruction. I know what it's like to be thrown a task and have no one break down exactly what it is that I am supposed to do. When I'm working with a young person, I never assume that they have prior knowledge of the job or how it is supposed to be executed. I make a point of carefully explaining what it is that I need and why I'm doing what I'm doing. I do not bark orders. I do not expect them to get me coffee the way Amanda Priestly does in that classic bitchy boss movie, *The Devil Wears Prada*. I don't make my interns pick up my dry cleaning or babysit my children. I respect that they are there to learn, so I try and assign them to meaningful tasks.

I go out of my way to treat them as if they are valued members of my company, which they may be one of these days, since I like to hire from within.

It is not always easy. In fact, I have an intern right now who is trying my commitment to not being a bitchy boss. I recently asked this young woman to put together an updated list of local bookstores and book reviewers at area magazines for a client campaign we are launching. She started giving me the information without having organized or vetted it. I was not happy with her performance, and I called her into my office to talk. In a very kind and patient voice, I explained to her that what I had assigned to her may have sounded mundane and boring but that it was crucial to our servicing the client to the best of MB's ability. I pointed out that the information that she had been asked to gather was a first step to getting this particular author booked on local TV and radio shows. As nicely as I could, I let her know that it was extremely important that the information she turned in be accurate, well-organized, and verified. Afterward, she went back to her desk and did a great job delivering on what I had asked of her. I never would have gotten that result if I had not been so patient. You may not always want to take the time like I did, but you absolutely must. That is the best way to get the most out of team members, especially when they are just starting out.

No matter how busy you are, you must put in the time and there is no way around it. For instance, I have an employee who is a great writer, but his press releases read a whole lot more like essays than actual media pitches. Reporters and producers are busy people who are deluged with information every day. They basically glance at what people send them and make split-second decisions about whether they are interested or not. It is imperative that we give them the information they need to make a good judgement quickly and succinctly. Getting all literary on them is a wasted effort. Instead of explaining all of this verbally to him, I sat down and spent thirty minutes writing out the press release myself. I didn't want to but felt I could do a better job of showing him instead of telling him what I wanted. Plus, that way he could have it and refer back to what I had written for other pitches. I emailed the rewritten release to him and told him that he could come into my office and talk about it if he wanted to. Do I have time to do this? No, but at the end of the day, that is the only way that your employees are going to improve. As for that employee, he has improved so much, and his writing is much better now.

When working with young employees, put yourself in their shoes and never forget how it was when you were just starting out. I will always remember how it was with me back when I was an excited but nervous recent college graduate. After graduating from Hofstra University in 1996, I wound up at the now-defunct Adelphia Cable, where I got paid only $9 an hour. I did not care about how little I earned because I considered that first TV news job my graduate education. I never would have gotten the better jobs in TV that came later if I hadn't had that experience. That's why I believe so strongly that interns and other young talent need someone to take a chance on them and help them get their start. I feel like it's my duty, frankly, to teach them, and it's yours as a manager or business owner as well. If they are giving us their time and they're dedicated and they're showing up every day, then we have to make sure that they are learning, evolving, and growing, not plateauing. I have two interns now, and I nurture them very much in the same way that I nurtured Jenna all those years ago. Never treat them like peons, as if all they are good for is to go get lunch or run other errands. Take the time to help them. I know you are busy. I am busy myself. There are many days when I don't talk to the interns all day, but I always make it a point to do regular check ins to see how they're doing. No matter what I have going on, I try to listen and understand their concerns as well as their hopes and expectations. I ask about their schools, the classes they are taking, and why they picked public relations. It's awkward when you are coming into a professional setting when you're a college student. I want them to know that I am there to help them just as much as they are there to help me. I never got paid for my internships, and I don't pay them. I consider their payment is all they will learn. I will reimburse them if they have to travel to a photo shoot or a TV station, but that's the extent of it. You get a better-quality intern when it's an unpaid position, because people don't look at it like a part-time job. They come in knowing that the only reason that they are there is to learn!

Make sure they are getting to know your company—the good, the bad, and the ugly. I'll never forget a former intern, Sam, who is now my firm's creative director. We met over the internet, but on his first day at MB and Associates, he was sitting at his desk when I walked in. I walked in, introduced myself, and welcomed him, since I hadn't been around for a few days. I was wearing super high-heeled wedge sandals, and when I walked away from his desk, I tripped and went flying into an armoire. I made a joke about being klutzy, and he told me later that it had set him at ease more than anything else I could have done. I was glad because you don't want your people intimidated by you. You need them to be confident team players. I was blessed in my youth, and I want to share my blessings with others. It takes one good day in an office to impact someone's life. Just one positive comment can ignite a fire in someone and change them forever. You can give your newbies the wings to fly, or you can clip their wings and they'll stay on the ground. My employees past and present need to be able to soar once they leave me.

One day, when I am retired and sunning myself in Florida, I want to look back and know that there are competent, efficient people living in this world and that I had a part in making them successful. I was gifted great mentors throughout my career, and I still have mentors today. So, take the time and help your interns and young employees develop. They picked your company as a place where they wanted to grow and learn. Make time for them. You don't have to invite them for a sit-down lunch every single day. That's totally unrealistic, but it is your duty to answer their questions. We all need to do our part in molding the next generation. I took a chance with Jenna all those years ago. She has paid me back tenfold. She is an incredible asset for MB and Associates and one of my dearest friends I lean on for love and light. None of that would have been possible had I been a bitch boss.

Don't Be a Bitch Bullets #5

Be a Meaningful Mentor

✓ *Show don't tell. Master writer Ernest Hemingway is the known source for this advice. He meant that a story is better when you show things instead of just saying them. When you illustrate what you mean, the recipient is more likely to buy into it and learn.*

✓ *Use the Socratic method to get your mentee to arrive at the conclusion you're hoping for. Asking specific questions will lead them onto the correct path, and if they think they arrived onto it with their own maneuvering, they're more likely to take the solution seriously.*

✓ *Listen up! Properly listening requires complete concentration. To be an effective listener, you need to pay attention to not only the words but the way in which they're said. Once you've garnered solid information, you can then offer the most concrete advice and your mentee will feel confident that you understand their point of view.*

✓ *Lead by example. Always follow this protocol: lead as I say and as I do. You'll earn respect, you'll "show" your mentee the proper process, and you'll show your team that you are a team player.*

Set shared goals. Don't just give your mentee goals and deadlines that you expect they meet; work with them to identify what they hope to achieve and help them to set realistic timelines that everyone is comfortable with.

Me and Jenna Stark

Me and Jaimi Blackburn

Me and Janet Zappala

Me and Rick Williams

Me reporting from Ground Zero on 9/12/2001

My children: Julian and Arielle Lichterman

MB and Associates team, spring 2021: (clockwise from top) Me, Sam Brownell, Semray Onal, Jeff Powell, Rachel Morales, Caron Jackson

Me and Heather Summerville

Chapter 6

YOU'VE GOTTA GO!

"Be a woman in business, not in everybody's business."

–Unknown

One of the things we do best at MB and Associates Public Relations is help our clients maintain their company's social media platforms. Back when this was still a relatively new area of expertise for us, I hired an assistant named Alyssa. Her job was simple: post something online every day about what our office had done. It could be a snapshot from a fashion shoot that we organized for one of the boutiques we represented, or sometimes she would link to an inspirational quote. At the time, we did not schedule posts in advance as we do now. Nor did I make a practice of screening individual posts before they went live. What a big mistake that turned out to be! I soon discovered that Alyssa had been posting misspelled words and had even created her own language that no one understood except her. It was bad. The worst, as we looked ridiculous! For instance, Alyssa described a menu item for one of our restaurant clients as being "dilummy." (She merged the words "delicious" and "yummy" to create this new vocabulary.) I was so embarrassed. I said to her, "Oh my God, that has to come down." On top of that, Alyssa was extremely moody. That's a big problem in the public relations industry. In this field, people must be "on" at all times. If I am having a bad morning and my kids are not cooperating or I have a boyfriend issue, I brush those things aside and put my game face on when I'm in the office or out somewhere dealing with a client. I expect my employees to do the same, and for the most part, they do. But with Alyssa I never knew what to expect from one day to the next. Either she was going to be a ray of sunshine or a massive thunderstorm. This affected my mood as well as everyone else's. On top of that, she was disrespectful and late finishing tasks. We are a small team. I like having a close-knit group. But when you are a small organization and you have a bad seed like her in the mix, everybody suffers. Things were always tense when she was around. My employees complained constantly, "She did this," or, "She did that." As time went on, I realized that Alyssa was not cut out to be in public relations. She belonged in a cubicle somewhere, not interacting with the public. I was honest with her about how things were going and put her on probation. I told her that I really wanted her to improve, which was true. Hiring and training a new employee is a long process and when you are a small business owner like I am, time is money. After you have invested all that energy into bringing a new person on board, you want things to work out. On the day that I finally let Alyssa go, I gave her the news as gently as I could. Even though I kept my voice calm, it was a charged situation. I got the distinct feeling that she wanted to punch me in my face, but I didn't back down. Unfortunately, when you own a company or are a manager of one, dismissing underperformers is part of the job. It's not easy. Trust me, I know. By nature, I am a people pleaser. I don't like to reprimand. I don't like to punish. I always like to give people more than one chance. Like a lot of female business owners, I tend to take on a mothering role with my employees and give them the benefit of the doubt. But after someone shows me that her heart isn't into her job or that she's not good at it, I will do what's necessary to protect my name, my company, and my other employees.

When I'm nervous about a firing, I envision my company as almost being a person instead of a corporation. I remind myself that I am protecting the company, its employees, and its assets. When I think of it that way, my mothering instinct kicks in and I find myself focusing on preserving the business at all costs, rather than feeling too sympathetic for the person who is getting let go. That gives me the courage and the strength to stand my ground even when I'm facing off with an upset former employee like Alyssa who I really think had been considering slugging me. The look on her face that morning pretty much said just that! If you are nervous about letting someone go, try to take the same approach. Remove yourself and your feelings from the equation. Focus instead on the brand that you worked so hard to build and your company. Think of all that would be lost if you do not do what needs to be done. Then, act decisively. I promise it will get easier.

Take the time a few years later, when I hired Sandi, who was model thin and had stunning, exotic good looks. She had long black hair hanging down her back and a happy, upbeat personality. She interviewed really well too. So, I was excited to offer her a job as my new assistant. But on her very first day of work, Sandi showed up with bright purple hair! I was speechless. I knew my fashion clients—boutique and spa owners—would love it, but my firm also handles public relations for conversative firms in finance and medicine. I teach my staff that we need to be chameleon-like when dealing with them and our other clients. If I go on a TV news shoot with one of our doctors or an attorney, I don't show up in the same exact outfit that I would wear if I were doing a segment with the owner of a trendy store or a jeweler. You dress to suit the client. All of that went through my head the morning that Sandi came in for her first day with purple hair. You can't disguise something like that. She couldn't sit in the office all day with a hat on. Her desk was in the front of my office. She would be the first one clients saw when they came in. So, later that day I pulled her aside and told her, "Your hair is very pretty, Sandi, but I'm a little concerned. I don't know if my clients are going to really appreciate the color. It's very creative and artistic, but they are not all in that space." She took it well and told me that she would let it grow out. To her credit, Sandi began arranging her hair in different ways to mask it, but that was the first sign that she was not a good fit. Others quickly followed. We soon learned that Sandi was incapable of doing even the most basic office tasks. Plus, she had an annoying habit of constantly interrupting members of my team to ask questions. This went on all day long. "Can you help me do this? Can you help me do that?" Instead of trying to look for things herself, she would ask my other staff members for it. "Do you have so and so's email?" "Do you have so and so's phone number?" It was very disruptive! To make things worse, Sandi had no sense of business etiquette. On one of her first days, she actually brought her lunch into my office to eat. Mind you, I was hard at work on a media pitch, but did that stop her? No. She placed her food on my desk and said, "So, how it going?" I was irritated, but I didn't want to be rude. So, I indulged her for a few minutes and then tried to get back to working. But she then started peppering me with personal questions about my kids and my divorce. I engaged with her for maybe another ten minutes, and then I said, "I'm sorry, I really need to get back to this deadline." Instead of leaving like a normal person would have done, Sandi continued sitting there and eating. The final straw came on the day of a big photo shoot that we coordinated for a local newspaper that took place on the beach in Atlantic City, New Jersey. Instead of helping with the shoot back at the hotel like my other staffers did, she was missing in action. She preferred hanging around the models and photographers instead of doing the grunt work the rest of us were doing. The newspaper's editor even complained to me, saying how Sandi was very "different" than my other MB team members, in connection to her work ethic. I was beside myself! I had to agree, though. After that, I knew that I had to let her go. This time around, I did not overthink it.

I told her, "I just don't think this is a fit," and wished her the best of luck. She cried, and I felt bad, but I kept my head in the game, instead of my heart. I paid her a few weeks in severance pay. I was glad she was gone, and I felt good about how I handled things.

Female business owners sometimes make the mistake of thinking we need to be overly harsh at times like this just to be perceived as strong. But that's just not true. I don't think you should act bitchy. Being nice and having good intentions with people has helped me immensely both professionally and personally. With my co- parent and the father of my two children, I approach it as if it were a business relationship. I try and take the emotion out of our conversations when things get heated. I do the same thing in professional settings. Instead of leading with emotion, which women tend to do because that is the way we are wired, we really need to think with our heads. We need to remember we are smart enough and strong enough and that we do not need to act bitchy to get the results that we are seeking, even when we are pushed. And believe me, people will push you!

Take Allison. She had been an on-air reporter in Florida and had come to MB and Associates with about fifteen years of broadcasting experience. I brought her on part-time. She was a good writer. She got good placements in the media. But like Alyssa, she would often show up for work in a bad mood. I would overhear her on the phone speaking rudely to our clients too. Then, one day she rolled in thirty minutes late and staggering like she had swallowed an entire bottle of vodka. When I asked if she was okay, Allison informed me that since she hadn't been able to sleep the night before, she had taken an Ambien. Since she appeared to be still under the influence of the sleeping aid, I did what any boss would do and suggested that she take a sick day. She snapped at me, saying, "I'm fine." Obviously, she wasn't, but as a boss, it's always wise to pick your battles, which I decided to do. I went back into my office and tried to let it go, but a little while later, I was copied on an email that Allison had sent to a reporter. It was full of misspellings, which just wouldn't do. I decided that it would be best if Allison went home for the rest of the day. I didn't feel like getting into it with her. I had a really important lunch meeting scheduled for later that day with the editor of a local magazine, and I knew what I had to do. So, I called Allison into my office. When she came in, I expected her to sit down in a chair facing my desk. But Allison, who is a bigger woman than me, came up and stood behind me. It felt intimidating, but I took a deep breath and said, "Allison, I think you should go home today. You are misspelling things in your emails, and I heard you slurring on the phone." She got angry and told me that she wasn't leaving. Something inside me snapped, and I shot back, "Not only are you leaving, but you can pack your stuff up and you can go permanently. You're fired! Go home!" I swear there was a long pause and that she was contemplating punching me just like I think Alyssa had. Luckily, she didn't. But she stood over me and stared me down like she was about to. Instead of jumping up like I wanted to, I remained in my chair and held her gaze. I didn't look away. I didn't back down. I meant business, and everything about my body language communicated that. Luckily, the situation didn't escalate, which it easily could have. But one thing

I didn't do that morning that I suggest that *you* do: try and have another employee in the room with you during intense situations. That person can act as a witness in case a former employee circles back and accuses you of having behaved improperly. Also, I allowed myself to be in a vulnerable position that day by remaining seated and having someone considerably larger than I am hovering over me. What if she had done what she was likely thinking and attacked me? You can avoid that by having security or at least another employee for backup on standby.

I don't believe in hiring friends, but I took a chance more than a decade ago on someone I had known for years. We had worked at two different TV stations together and had become really close. Jane even was a bridesmaid in my wedding. So, I ignored a nagging feeling telling me not to bring her on and hired her anyway. For a while it was fine, even though it sometimes felt awkward managing her. Jane had really strong ties with the local media, which was a big asset to MB and Associates. Plus, she was fun to have around the office. The first sign that trouble might be looming came after I announced an incentive plan to reward employees who brought in new business. I discussed it with her one day during a coffee meeting. Her response? "Why would I want to do that? It's just going to create more work for me." I was taken aback. Business development was a big part of her job description, and she knew that. But because she was my friend and I didn't want any friction, I shrugged it off, which turned out to be a really big mistake. Jane had begun doing some odd things. She was on the phone with personal calls a great deal. I noticed that when she got a call on her cell phone, Jane would take it outside of our offices in the hallway. This happened several times a day. That made me raise my eyebrow a little bit, but, again, I shrugged it off. Then, there was the day we were meeting with a physician client and I made a minor mistake about the time a segment we had filmed would air on the news. Jane yelled out, "No, that's wrong!" I was embarrassed, but I also got the feeling that she was trying to get this doctor to want to work with *her* instead of with me. I remember wondering, "What are you trying to do? Take my client?" I was irate. In business you must be united with your team members and cover each other's backs. Had the circumstances been switched, I would never have conducted myself that way. I would have made the correction without making Jane look bad in front of a client. If one of the team looks bad, we all look bad. That's a cardinal rule in business! Afterward, I pulled her aside and said, "That meeting went well, but you can never do that to me again. I would never do that to you, and you cannot do that to me. Don't throw me under the bus in front of a client." Jane apologized, but I knew something was up. I was reluctant to let her go, though, because we were friends and I didn't want drama. But I knew what I needed to do. The next morning, Jane had a shoot at a TV station in Philly, and when she came back, I nervously called her into my office and told her I was laying her off. I used the excuse of having lost a big client earlier that month, which was true, and she shot back, "Why am I the one being fired?" I responded, "You're not being fired. You're being laid off because you make the most money. I need to let you go." I didn't really want to get into all of the things that had led up to my decision. I wanted to tell her it was because of how she had backstabbed me during a meeting with a client, that she was not a team player, and that she was spending more time on her cell phone in the hallway than at her desk. I could have rattled off all of these things, but I really wanted to take the high road. Besides, it was awkward because she was my friend. So, she went into her office to pack up. As she was slowly preparing to go, I had her email forwarded to me. I spotted one thanking her for her service at a spa that we didn't represent. I recall thinking, "That's strange." I went into the office she was cleaning and said, "I just got this email from so and so. What is that about?" Jane started talking quickly and saying that she had won a raffle for a free day at the spa. It was obviously a lie. She left shortly after that.

I couldn't shake the nagging feeling that something else was going on. That night I stayed late and combed through her work email. I was stunned to find hundreds of emails and media pitches for clients that our firm did not represent. I could not believe what I had discovered. Jane had been running her own PR firm from the offices of MB and Associates PR! Now I had a legal issue on my hands. The next day, my remaining staff and I went through Jane's computer and found all kinds of representation contracts between her and various local businesses. I also was stunned to discover that she had an adult son that no one ever knew existed. I felt betrayed, and I wound up suing her for breach of contract, fraud, and unjust enrichment. I didn't want to, but I did it to protect my company. We wound up settling out of court. Somehow an item about the ordeal running from my offices wound up in the gossip pages of our local newspaper, which did not paint Jane in a very good light. Karma! Needless to say, Jane and I are no longer friends.

Even though I got my revenge with Jane, I despise confrontation. I shy away from it like the plague. If I have to face it, I face it, but I don't seek out drama. Some people do, but not me. I don't want it in my office, and if you're reading this book, then I suspect that you don't want it either. You don't have to be ruthless and walk all over your employees to be successful. If you think that's what it takes to get ahead, you couldn't be more wrong. Early on in my career, I worked under a few bosses from hell and it was awful. When I became a business owner, I vowed never to treat my employees the way that I had been treated. Not only do I *not* have it in me to be cruel, I would never want to work in that kind of environment. Although there are plenty of examples of successful bitchy business owners, their employees most likely despise them. Walking into their workspaces, you can feel the tension. I would never want to work in a toxic environment like that again and I don't want my staff to either. It's bad for business. Smart business owners and managers know that you get much more out of a happy team than one that is miserable.

Don't Be a Bitch Bullets #6

Giving the Ax with Authority

✓ *Meet face to face. Always terminate an employee in person. It's the most courteous and professional form of communication when letting an employee go.*

✓ *Wave the red flags. Give the employee ample warning. Consider a written review, a formal critique, and a chance to improve before severing ties.*

✓ *There is power in numbers. Always have another present before you start the termination conversation. Always. Having another present will protect you from possibly getting sued, and you'll have a second voice if dialogue gets dicey.*

✓ *Keep it short and sweet. There is no need to make the conversation any longer than necessary. If you've previously expressed dismay over job performance and provided them ample time for improvement, there is no need to rehash inadequacies.*

✓ *Once fired, they must depart the premises immediately. Don't permit a fired employee to speak with your team or access their desk unaccompanied.*

Chapter 7

MISTAKES VS. MISSTEPS: DON'T CONFUSE THE TWO!

"If somebody can do something 80 percent as good as you think you would have done it yourself, then you've got to let it go."

–Sara Blakely, Spanx founder

There is nothing worse than having to repeat yourself. I'll say that again. There is nothing worse than having to repeat yourself! I mean, really! When taking the time to explain a situation, plan of attack, and intended solution to a team, an employee, even your own kids, only to have it utterly ignored or simply forgotten really gets me fired up. Yes, I do get angry, because what I really want to convey to the guilty party would not be feminine, certainly not empathetic, and not kind. So, I don't. More often than not, the person who lost the message (likely in translation) had no ill intentions. The information may have gone over their head, they may have been distracted at the time of communication, or they simply may have been afraid to share that they didn't fully understand, knowing full well they were utterly clueless. Another key culprit I often encounter in leading a team is when a team member acts on his feet but chooses the wrong path. He thought he was being wise; he thought the outcome would lead to a victory, but instead he got the company in hot water, angered a client, or possibly even severed a relationship. All equally bad. But here's the thing: you can't freak out. Even though you may want to rip your hair out and scream at the top of your lungs from the highest mountain top, you simply cannot. You need to instead smile softly, breathe deeply, and listen. Listen to their reasoning, listen to their mindset, and listen to their explanation. Don't! Freak! Out!

I encountered one such situation not that long ago. One of the many components of a client's PR campaign is influencer marketing. Since the advent of social media, we have been thrown into the folds of this digital marketing for client branding. I wholeheartedly still believe that what I call "mainstream media" is the most beneficial and it is where we spend our greatest focus, but there's no question that what these Instagram public figures say and do has impact. So, on one such social media campaign, we reached out to a lovely lifestyle influencer from the Philadelphia region to visit our firm's dermatologist client for a treatment. I delegated these duties to my assistant and knew that my manager and lead on this particular account would be overseeing the process to ensure all went smoothly. The influencer, who was plus-sized, asked for a treatment she was not a candidate for. The treatment was called Emsculpt, and like CoolSculpt—which freezes your fat—it works to cure a small pocket of fat that can't be properly addressed at the gym or by dieting alone. Very different from a liposuction procedure, this treatment is meant to simply tone an area, not really create a dramatic result. So, the treatment would not have been able to give this particular body type any real result, which would have ended badly for both my client, my firm, and the influencer. Unlike my assistant, who doesn't work in this particular client's scope of work on a regular basis, my manager knew the ins and outs and of this treatment and who it was best suited for, but drew his own conclusion (without any input from the doctor) that it would work to some degree and be okay. Huge mistake. Massive!

On the day of the treatment, the influencer took off of work, excitedly showing up at my client's office for what she thought was going to be a great day. She thought she'd leave with a flatter tummy, more toned for the upcoming summer months of bathing suits and fitted sundresses, and my client would receive great content as she documented her journey and experience. But what happened instead was a catastrophic public relations disaster. As the medical assistant at my client's practice assessed her, she was left dumbfounded. What to do? She trusted my office to ensure we'd be sending the right candidate for the procedure, and my office had dropped the ball. Taking things into his own hands, my manager ultimately caused a perfect storm, which is also my responsibility as the owner of the company, to say the least. The physician's assistant called my cell phone in a panic, unsure of how to handle this very uncomfortable situation. She did not want to offend the influencer who was her patient but also knew that proceeding with the treatment would make no sense. I told her to blame my office in order to save face for their practice and share that we had a miscommunication with her and made a mistake setting up this treatment. I told her to offer her something else that would benefit her and make sure she left happy. It wasn't an ideal solution but, in the moment, it seemed the only right thing to do.

When speaking with my assistant and my manager, I learned about his conscious decision to make his own medical analysis that the treatment would indeed work. I explained how incorrect that act was and the jeopardy he ultimately put my client's brand in as well as our own. Instead, I explained, he should have consulted the doctor for his professional opinion rather than simply diagnosing the situation himself. He agreed after much back and forth and ultimately realized my stance was on point. Next, to smooth over the situation with the influencer. I needed to personally apologize as the owner of the PR firm and make sure she didn't have any uneasy feelings about my client. That to me was most important. I also cared about her feelings and wanted to make sure she was content with the outcome. I'm very thankful I took that step to reach out to her, despite my very intense day and back-to-back meetings on my schedule. I left her a very heartfelt message on her voicemail and shared my personal cell number for her to call at her convenience, explaining how concerned I was that she had borne the brunt of a horrible mistake made by my office and that I personally wanted to make things up to her. When she called me back, I patiently listened to her as she shared her feelings of embarrassment and upset about the day's events. I could hear she was fighting back tears and that made my heart sink. As a women's empowerment advocate and also a kind soul, I'd never want to be responsible for someone else's pain. I softly spoke to her, apologizing, explaining how incredible she was (She is!) and how this one unpleasant office visit should not make her feel any less or unworthy. She listened and thanked me for my time and care, and I promised her that when she returned for another treatment—a treatment that would be perfect for her—I'd join her. She was grateful and my client was too. That's what a boss who's not a bitch does. I didn't scream and rant to my manager. I addressed the situation. I was stern with him. I explained his downfall and my deep disappointment with his decision-making process and hoped that he'd take it all into account and act differently next time.

It was a frustrating situation and tested my trust of my team. My first thought was to take over the influencer marketing or have a larger role in overseeing the day-to-day process of it. But that's not a productive solution. If I can't trust my team and fill the need to take over tasks to ensure they're done properly, then I might as well take over an employee's entire job in the process. And leaders who are fixers wind up with teams that are weak. I'm still growing and evolving in this department. It's much easier to solve a problem than to seek a solution from an employee. But if you want an independent, confident, and efficient group, you need to step back. Let them fall, help break the crash, and dust them off so they can fly the next time.

Studies show that punishing an employee for making a mistake can destroy your business. Employees already start their workdays fueled with fear of making a costly mistake, so many will avoid taking a risk. When your employees fear making a mistake, they will underachieve and underperform. And that is a curse to a company! Instead, your team needs to be confident so they can be bold and fearless. Like the teachable lesson my manager learned from the poor judgment he practiced with the influencer debacle, mistakes are useful. A report published in *Scientific American* says that our mind actually expands when we learn from mistakes. Our brains build pathways that can lead to success if we leverage the information learned from a situation. Mistakes, while misfortunes, are unintentional. They're simply the result of one sizing up a situation and going in the wrong direction. Mistakes also can lead to milestones. In order to embrace the error and sway my employees toward a path of productivity, I use these tactics: First, I make sure I have a safety net in place. Just like most of us, I had an invisible web beneath me at all times, thanks to the confidence and nurturing I felt from my parents growing up, and your employees need that sense of security too. They need to feel safe in order to enter the dangerous territory of risk-taking. In order to cultivate this dynamic, I meet with my team members frequently, seeking their input and utilizing each one's unique strengths in the trusting and engaging environment I always strive to create. This way, I know my employees will feel less pressure to avoid making mistakes. I allow my team to use their voice. Whether it's in collaboration with the rest of our office or with the client, I always ask them to weigh in. Sometimes, depending on the premise of a client meeting, I will also let them lead the dialogue while I support them. I do this so they feel comfortable and confident to speak up. Sequestering an employee prevents them from adding value. When you encourage your employees to take risks, you help them produce and develop their skillset and expand without fear of backlash.

Another move I make on a regular basis is to honor my own errors. No one is perfect, including the boss, and we all can learn and grow, each and every day. Employees will unequivocally feel safer to make a mistake if they see you do too. I will always share my own mistakes and what I've learned and how I will alter my actions in the future. When bosses cover their tracks, they create an uneasy workplace. If you're open, they'll be more candid, and the team will thrive as a result. Be open and honest so you can authentically propel.

Lastly, make sure they understand it's okay to make a mistake. Without reprimand, just like the instance with my manager and the influencer mess up, I told him to admit his wrongdoing to the client, as did I, and we found a solution to fix the problem. I'm confident this client now trusts us even more because we were honest about the missteps, rather than creating a larger fiasco by dancing around the error.

Just don't confuse a mistake with irresponsibility. That's grounded in consistent carelessness and was the root of a massive mistake an employee caused me in the fall of 2007. At that time, I was about five years into owning MB and Associates and we were really working with all the high-end lifestyle experts in the greater Philadelphia region. We represented the best jewelers, hair salon and spas, women's fashion boutiques, and aesthetic medicine experts. One of our ultra-chic clients was a famous bridal boutique called Suky, nestled in the heart of affluent Main Line Philadelphia. Suky was where you went if you were a bride-to-be and had no real budget hindering your pocketbook. A local Mecca for all things Vera Wang, the robust store stood dripping in white satins, ivory silks, and sparking crystal chandeliers throughout. It was elegance at its finest, and I was proud to represent the brand. Working on behalf of this bridal salon gave me clout on the PR spectrum, and the owner was so much fun to work with; her business was very easy to pitch and secure media coverage for, since it was so incredibly famous. You could say it was a dream client. After working with the brand for about a year and securing a ton of local press to boot, I secured the owner a segment on iVillage, a nationally syndicated midday talk show on the NBC network, to speak about the hottest wedding gown trends for the season. The show was broadcast live, out of their Chicago station (where Jerry Springer shoots his talk show). Because the owner and I had to travel there (myself or a team member always accompanies clients to TV segments to facilitate on-site), with five twentyish-pound wedding gowns plus our own luggage, it made the most sense to source the models locally and not have to fly them there. While I had coordinated the segment with my client with regards to her gown selection and speaking points, I left the model roundup task up to one of my associates. We will call her "Jennifer." Now, keep in mind, this sort of thing was very routine for my office, and for Jennifer. Sourcing models was something we did almost weekly for the many fashion and lifestyle clients we represented. The only catch was that our model roster was based in Philadelphia, New York, and Washington, D.C., where we did the most press at the time, and Jennifer had become notorious as of late for taking shortcuts, which had my eyebrows raised.

Chicago wasn't a city we often worked in at the time, so model connections there were not yet intact. Jennifer knew the type of women we needed to wear the gowns to showcase them in the strongest light and exude confidence on live television. She knew what she was to look for. So, I figured she would do some due diligence and book us five attractive, diverse, and confident women for this very important segment. I trusted her, and I wasn't worried about her judgment. Jennifer had that part of the project under control, I assumed, and I could focus on the rest of the very involved facilitation. Was I in for a surprise! On the afternoon the day before the shoot, my client and I headed out to the airport together but soon saw that getting to Chicago would be an absolute disaster. Upon our arrival to the airport, it was one catastrophe after the next. First, (as I mentioned, the gowns were incredibly heavy), we had issues checking them in. That created a great deal of aggravation and stress, due to some confusion about paying for extra poundage, but we got the job done. Then, it was off to our gate. We planned to fly out at 4 p.m., which had us landing in Chicago at about 5 p.m. central time so we would be able to have a nice, early dinner and get a good night's sleep. We planned to get up at the crack of dawn in order to be at the station for the 4 a.m. call-time. The show went live at 9 a.m., and we needed to get the models dressed, rehearse with them walking in the gowns, and get my client prepped and camera-ready for her big segment, as she would be interviewed by the show host about the trends and speak to the looks each woman modeled down the studio's catwalk.

First hiccup: the plane was delayed by an hour. Not a big deal. We decided to grab a bite at the airport and enjoyed a glass of red wine, unwinding and chatting in a carefree fashion about the next day's segment. As we sipped our pinot noir and shared a flatbread pizza, we laughed and exchanged business stories and strategies with one another. Then, at about 7 p.m. it was time to board our flight. We planned that after landing at O'Hare Airport, obtaining the checked wedding gowns, catching a cab, and heading into our Magnificent Mile hotel, we'd likely be in our rooms by 9 p.m., leaving us plenty of time to settle in and get enough sleep, so we didn't look ragged for TV. Sigh.

This time, we boarded the plane without a delay, but were left idling on the tarmac. The minutes ticked by ever so slowly. We'd glance at one another, wondering when we were going to take off. No one was updating us, and nothing was happening. What was going on? An hour went by, and then the pilot finally came on the loudspeaker to share that the flight had been canceled due to a technical malfunction. OMG. With that, I went into full panic mode, because we had to get to Chicago! There was no way, at that point, we could cancel. If we had done so, we'd be leaving the producer with a wide gap of unfilled airtime on a national show, and I was sure that my chances of ever booking another segment there would be zero. My client also wanted to try and salvage the situation, since it was a huge business opportunity for her, as her gorgeous gowns were to be modeled by exquisite women—so many brides-to-be all over the US would surely reach out to her to place their orders after viewing them live. We had to make it work! Somehow, we had to get there.

Racing off the plane, we dashed down to baggage claim to grab the twenty pounds of dead bridal gown weight and fled to the airline's front desk. No more flights were left on the airline we were booked on, but after research and lots of phone calls, a very helpful attendant managed to book us on another airline on the other side of the airport. It was departing in thirty minutes, and it was the last flight out for the night. I'm almost certain passersby must have thought we were completely crazy as we sprinted, dressed in chic work dresses and stilettos, through the airport terminals, dragging the gowns and our luggage the entire way. I felt beads of sweat drip down my temples, and I was definitely panting as I made my way, but I was determined we'd get to the gate and make it on for the 10 p.m. departure to Chi Town. Sweating and clutching our freshly printed paper tickets, we laughed at the utter chaos of the entire ordeal. But we made it. And as we sat down and got buckled in, I was sure that we had just encountered the worst of the trip. How could things get any worse?

As we took off with the glowing skyline of Philadelphia trailing behind, we decided to close our eyes. After all, we'd need all the rest we could get. By the time we were to arrive at our hotel, it would be close to midnight, and the wake-up call was only a few hours from then. So, we'd only really get about five hours of sleep, but at least we'd make it to the station and the segment would go on.

I don't recall if I actually slept on that flight, but I do remember stepping off the plane, retrieving the gowns, and hailing a cab in a bit of a fog. Exhausted and stressed, all I wanted to do was shower and get into bed so I could have my wits about me the next day and be on my top game for this national TV spot. However, I didn't account for the massive ironing that awaited both of us upon check in. My client was planning to tackle that all herself, but with the late arrival time, I offered to pitch in and took half of her silk heap with me to my hotel room. The delicate fabric on the ball gowns had been tightly packed in garment bags, making them severely creased, wrinkled, and honestly unattractive upon unpacking them. Finally, at 1 a.m., my head crashed into the pillow. I fell asleep in less than twenty minutes and woke up two hours later to a pounding on my door. My client and I had requested a 3 a.m. wake-up call so that we could shower, dress, and primp before our 4 a.m. studio arrival. But that too had gone awry. Stumbling out of bed, I thought I was having a nightmare, but as I whipped the door open, I could see my client was freaking out! "They didn't call! They didn't call us!" She was screaming and looked like she may cry. I glanced at my phone. It was 3:45 am. Now I knew I was having a nightmare and living it in the flesh. "Bird bath!" I shouted back, looking at her squarely, my eyes suddenly wide open. She knew exactly what I meant. No time to shower, no time to shave our legs, no time to even brush our hair. Forget the makeup. I literally hopped in and out of the water—more of a mist washing—almost in the same motion. I shoved my arms into my dress, thrust my legs into black tights, and literally ran my fingers through my hair as a comb. All done!

We ran down the hall, now sweating carrying the twenty-pound gowns, which were hanging on garment bag hangers dangling from our fingers, and jumped into a cab. Deep breath. "This too shall pass," I kept saying silently, as a mantra. I was sure the adrenaline from this heightened stress ordeal would keep us full of energy at least until 9:30 a.m., when we'd be off the air and we could crash. As we climbed out of the cab and glanced up at the skyscraper before us, I could see the sun peeking through the clouds. It was the start of a gorgeous, crisp fall day in downtown Chicago. The view and the air eased my quick-paced heartbeat a bit, and I started to feel more calm as we walked up the exterior stairway into the glass building. Then, I glanced to my right and zoned in on five women standing by the entranceway. Could they be the models Jennifer hired? They didn't look like the tall, elegant professionals we usually worked with. My firm's go-to models were typically not especially seasoned, as all were just starting their careers. The women who usually modeled for us were on their way to becoming top regional models and were happy to obtain as much experience on-camera as possible. They were thrilled to work pro-bono for us in exchange for an incredible experience and television clips to use on their resumes. It was always a win-win situation all-around.

As we got closer, I could see that the ladies appeared to be waiting for someone, and when I heard one say my name, I wanted to die. We were supposed to meet the models my associate booked at the front entrance, so we could all walk in with the credentials the producer shared with us. Once again, I stood panic-stricken on the inside but cool and collected for all to see. I've always been good at hiding my stress in front of clients or media. I guess it's from all my days in news when I'd be scrambling to put a story together and have to instantly go live, speaking calmly and informatively, zoning in fully on the task ahead. Those skills came in especially handy when all hell was breaking loose.

"Hi, are you Mindie?" one of the tattoo-covered, blue-haired women from the pack inquired. OMG. These *were* the models! Not only was it obvious that they wouldn't be able to fit into these slim-fitting gowns, only suited for the typical runway physique, these ladies looked rough. And I don't mean rough around the edges. I mean they looked as if they could have been strong candidates for a motorcycle gang. My client looked like she might faint, as she met my eyes. This could not be happening! Not only would they be poor representations of my client's brand, but they'd also never be able to fit into the gowns. This was yet another nightmare! As my client and I stood by the entranceway, weighted down by the gowns, which were now out of the garment bags, freshly ironed and in all of their puffery, I racked my brain trying to figure out what I was going to do. I secretly wished my client hadn't woken up on her own and instead slept through the segment. My hands were visibly shaking, and I was completely confused. I was irate with Jennifer for hiring non-model models for such an important segment, but I told myself that I would deal with that later. I smiled and thanked the women for coming, and kindly inquired which agency they were with. Another one of the ladies, a bubbly twenty-something with white, frosty-spiked hair started to laugh. "We're not with no agency," she explained. "We answered an ad on Craigslist." "Craigslist?" I asked. I thought I must have misheard her. "Yes, the ad for free models for a TV show." Now, to say I was livid with Jennifer would be an understatement. How utterly dumb of her to post an ad on a site that was not only for novices but not even an industry professional platform! I was horrified. But the show had to go on—literally.

My client looked disgusted, and I could tell by the color of her face, incredibly angry. She was furious with me, and I couldn't blame her. Although I had not personally booked these models, my associate had and, therefore, her mistake was my mistake and I needed to own it. I always own it. I told my client I was profusely sorry and that I would handle things. I told her to go into hair and makeup and just relax and focus on the speaking points she would share on air. I then brought her a cup of coffee from the green room (which I also desperately needed) and returned to the entranceway to dismiss the "models" as nicely as I could. I apologized to them, explaining that while I was most grateful that they made the trip in, that there was some confusion at my office back in New Jersey and they were no longer needed for the segment. I then offered to pay for their cab fare and added in some extra money so that I could treat them to break-fast. They were nice about it, but I still felt bad. There was no way they could have served my client in this segment, but it was an awkward situation, and I certainly didn't want to hurt anyone's feelings. Thankfully, that didn't appear to be the case.

Business isn't always easy, and it's not always warm and fuzzy. But you can be kind, and I was, as I waved goodbye. Now I had to find new models and in sixty minutes or less. The hunt was on, but first I found the show's producer and told her the truth. I apologized and explained the situation and how I had to dismiss the models my office had initially hired, as they would not have been a good fit for the segment. She understood and appreciated my honesty. Next, I asked her if there might be some attractive interns we could possibly borrow. Luckily, there was! Great, two models were secured. I scoured every corner of that station, going into other production studios hunting for pretty, fairly thin women who weren't too busy and could spare an hour to strut on a catwalk. I walked over to the Jerry Springer set and introduced myself to the production assistants who were setting up for the famous talk show host's afternoon taping. I gave them a quick overview of what I needed, and they both volunteered, assuring me that they had been on camera before and had plenty of time to help me and still do their jobs efficiently for Mr. Springer. Amazing! And with just one more spot to fill and no others to solicit, I volunteered myself. I do not think I'm a model, but I am a size two and am most comfortable on camera. I wasn't thrilled to appear on a national show as a model, as accomplished publicists rarely put themselves in any media a client is involved in, but I really felt I had no other choice. I needed this segment to be strong for my client and I know she really wanted to showcase all five of the looks we had hauled in from Philadelphia. I also owed it to the producer of the show. So, there I was needing a shower, sweating, and with uncombed hair about to appear on a national show in less than thirty minutes. As I plopped in the hair and makeup chair for a very fast hair brushing and lipstick swipe, I kept myself calm and focused; I told myself I'd address the model debacle with Jennifer after the segment was wrapped.

Before I knew it, we were in the brightly lit studio, standing on stage in the middle of a grand TV set, and each of us took our turn modeling our gown, smiling at the camera, and strutting our stuff. It was over in a flash, and my client was thrilled. She did well. She spoke with ease, laughed with the host, and smiled sweetly. No one at home would ever have known the drama that had unfolded just an hour before. That is the magic of TV, as well as the tactics of a fast-thinking publicist who can fix situations and keep the client calm. That's what we are there for, in addition to securing the media. Every good boss knows going above and beyond the job description is not only key, it's crucial.

Now, what to do with Jennifer? I wanted to have a serious conversation with her, but that would have to wait until I was back on the East Coast and in our offices. I also didn't want to get into a heated conversation with an employee in front of my client, and she and I needed to stay in close proximity as we still had the return trip back to Philadelphia ahead of us. I did call Jennifer to check in and explained I needed to find new models in a pinch and that I'd speak with her more about that when I returned to the office on Monday. I think she got my drift because I could hear her voice sort of tremble. She had gotten lazy in the last few months. Not consistently lazy, but enough so that I had noticed, and this time her laxity had caused a disaster. Thankfully, a disaster I was able to repair, but it was nonetheless unnecessary stress for my client and certainly unnecessary angst for me.

I was the first one into the office the following Monday morning. I planned it that way. I wanted to get my catch-up work out of the way so that I could focus solely on Jennifer when she arrived. After I heard her call out, "Good morning," I asked her to come into my office once she was settled. As she walked into my doorway, I welcomed her and asked her to close the door. She knew I meant business. I asked her to explain the steps she took in scouting out the models. Did she research agencies in Chicago, did she look at their portfolios, resumes, perhaps see any of the prior work they had done? We had taken those steps and more when sourcing models in the past. She had not. Instead, as she explained, not knowing Chicago well and unfamiliar with which agencies to call, she posted an ad on Craigslist hoping she'd score women who would be suitable. At that time, Craigslist was used often for a variety of jobs and other opportunities. In her defense, this was pre-Facebook, pre-Instagram, and not utterly out of the norm. However, her reasoning was that she didn't see the need to take the time to research modeling agencies and vet the models after they responded to her ad. That was inexcusable. That was careless, and that was not a mistake. That was a misstep. It was irresponsibility, and that kind of thing will cost you clients, tarnish your reputation, and sabotage your business. There is no room for that at MB and Associates and there should be no room for missteps and irresponsibility at your company either. Did I fire Jennifer? Well, not on that particular day. I instead put her on probation and told her she was in jeopardy of losing her job if she didn't pick up the pace and show me that her heart was in it to win it. As it turned out, it wasn't, and that's okay. I don't make mistakes twice. I give people chances to sharpen and shape up, and if they don't, they're gone. That's not being a bitch. *That* is being a boss!

Embrace Errors

✓ *Fancy failure. Failure is a critical component to success. You learn who you are, you learn what makes the world turn, and you obtain better solutions when you embrace failing.*

✓ *Figure out why you made the mistake to begin with. Where did the path begin to go awry? Ask what could you have done differently and etch the mental note into your memory for next time.*

✓ *Free your fear. You can't progress if you're afraid to take a risk. You must be brave enough to take a step and potential (second) mistake. Playing it safe only causes you to plateau and plummet.*

✓ *Own your error. Taking responsibility for your mistake is imperative. As soon as you take responsibility and hold yourself accountable, the learning process will escalate.*

✓ *Mistakes will motivate. After encountering an error, be open to feedback and look to reattempt the task with a new approach in place.*

Chapter 8

WHEN LIFE IS A BITCH

*"When you look at successful women, they have
other women who have supported them, and they've
gotten to where they are because of those women."*

–Sheryl Sandberg

Public relations does not have the reputation of being an overly friendly field, especially among female entrepreneurs. It's actually just the opposite. PR is infamous for being riddled with petty competition and women who are coined "nuts" by professional standards. It's a cutthroat, highly stressful, sometimes toxic, and often thankless field. Yes, I love it. But with so much cattiness, one could easily vomit. A prime example were the stories I shared working for Queen Bee, and trust me, I only tipped the iceberg! However, as icy as she was, Queen Bee is not alone in the sea of B. There are dozens, countless Queen Bees buzzing around, just like the one I once worked for. And they're not all in the world of PR. Bitches exist in nearly every corporate office throughout America. As any female in the workplace knows, women don't always like other women. In fact, many outright detest their female counterparts. I shy away from all that drama and clatter. I keep my eyes on the prize and my focus on my reflection in the mirror. I rise above that ill-infested ocean of mean girls and always put my best foot forward. It's professional, it's classy, and, for me, it's the only way to be.

About a year after officially founding MB and Associates and setting up my corporate name, I hired my first assistant and my intern, Jenna, to help me with day-to-day tasks. I had about ten clients at this time and was starting to receive real professional recognition from many in the industry. One afternoon, I was especially flattered when I received a call from a high-end magazine sales associate in Philadelphia who wanted to give me a referral. Her client, an elite women's apparel boutique in the beautiful town of Haddonfield, NJ (where I later set up my second office) was looking for a public relations professional to organize and facilitate monthly events in her store. She wanted to entertain her very top tier clientele in a special night full of fun, information, and, of course, shopping. The boutique, situated in the center of town, carried designer lines like Escada and Moschino and attracted women mostly over the age of forty. The storeowner wanted the event to be invite-only and solely for her customers as a thank you for their ongoing loyalty, as well as an incentive to come in and shop. It sounded fun and easy to organize. I was in! I met with the owner, Angela, at her boutique one early spring day to flesh out her ideas and add my own. We'd have an ongoing series of events for six months, featuring a guest expert at each event who would do a demonstration or offer some sort of insight about a fashion or beauty trend. I secured the trendy American cuisine restaurant and bar I was representing to serve as the event's sponsor. They would provide complimentary light fare for each event and in exchange market their restaurant specials and menu to the attendees, who were their ideal patrons. Angela would provide wine and soft drinks. Also on the agenda was a soft PR campaign to garner some interest from the media. Angela wanted to call the event "Girls Night Out," which to me sounded extremely flat and horribly boring. It was an ordinary name commonly used by bars and nightclubs for years. But I obliged, as she really liked the name, and it was her event after all.

After much planning and plotting, I launched the first "Girls Night Out" in early May with a plastic surgeon as the featured guest. The doctor performed a Restylane filler procedure on guests' labial folds (or smile lines). It was 2005, and there was still very little awareness about fillers and aesthetic medicine in general. Plastic surgery overall was still fresh and new. The women were fascinated, just watching the doctor do his thing. The demonstration was followed with a lot of questions from the seated guests. After that, much mingling, sipping, noshing, and shopping. Angela was ecstatic. She couldn't have been happier!

Immediately following the first "Girls Night Out," I began planning the next one. The second party featured an etiquette expert who spoke about party planning, family gatherings, and other functions where controversy can sometimes arise. That guest expert was a hit, and the attendees were thrilled with her advice and wisdom. Angela was so happy to host her beloved customers, and I could have sworn I saw a glimmer in her eye each time the credit card machine was swiped with another fabulous purchase from a happy shopper. Ca-ching! Other events followed that one, each occurring on the first Thursday of the month. I had Jenna in tow as my right-hand (wo)man to help with whatever was needed, and when she wasn't present, my assistant and only employee at the time, Jeanine, was there to help. With consideration of the rest of my daily workload—pitching the media and overseeing press opportunities—these events were cookie-cutter, easy breezy for me to successfully pull off. It was almost relaxing to be there and assist each month once the earlier organization and facilitation was done. The monthly events were starting to grab attention. Some lifestyle reporters had heard about it and reached out to me, and every fashionista in Haddonfield was talking about the local "Girls Night Out," even if they weren't on the coveted guest list. It was smooth sailing... until my ship hit an iceberg.

Not far from Haddonfield, just down the Garden State Parkway, about an hour east, sits Atlantic City. Glassy and impressive skyscrapers fill the landscape, bustling energy from lit-up casinos consumes the air, and scores of young people and high rollers make the city abuzz. Also, on the coast of the Atlantic Ocean, there was another type of "Girls Night Out" building momentum. This one was really a brilliant affair, but one I would never want to have been involved with. Although my Haddonfield account was indeed an "event," and I have facilitated and coordinated many events in my almost two decades in business, I do not pride myself on being an event planner. Event planning is grueling in ways that media strategy is not. It consists of ongoing, brutally long nights, unending grunt work, the need to pay constant attention to the most minute details pertaining to aesthetics, timing, and, of course, securing an impressive audience out of the air to be present at each and every party. That's simply not my lane. I don't really have a passion for any of that.

I love the media. I love to write. I love working one-on-one with people. I live to be an extension of the news and have the ability to utilize my degree in journalism. It gives me purpose. I'm not a party planner. I don't want to be a party planner, and there are better party planners to hire—like the woman who was spearheading the other "Girls Night Out." Notorious for being tough and running her company with an iron fist, this event planner was also in public relations, but her niche was definitely planning parties. She and I could not have been more different. We are polar opposites, both professionally and personally, and I'm not sorry to say that. Her "Girls Night Out" also consisted of a series of women's events but had an entirely different concept. First and foremost, it was open to the public. Her core market was twenty-somethings, and she was holding her "Girls Night Out" monthly events at different locations featuring different boutiques and restaurants, and with other industry leaders. It was a variety of multiple businesses all offering a sampling of what they were about to the young society of Atlantic City. It sounded like a lot of fun. I would have loved to have gone as a guest myself! The event-planning public relations firm was owned by a woman by the name of Celeste. I had never actually met Celeste, but I had heard of her, and it wasn't all good. Like Queen Bee, she, too, was infamous for making her employees cry. Rumor had it that the corners of her mouth would curl up a bit when the first tears of an employee would fall. I don't know why she was allegedly so mean, but my guess is that it was for the same reasons Queen Bee and so many others like her are too. They have their own insecurities and make for the ultimate "bitch boss." I was grateful that I not only had never worked for her, but I had also never worked *with* her. Hearing what I did of her workplace culture, I was certain she and I would not have meshed. That said, I did have a great deal of respect for her. One couldn't deny her success as a businesswoman. Even though I did not know her personally, whenever her name would come up in conversations with other associates, I would often pay her compliments to others. Why not? She was accomplished. She was smart, and she deserved it. Even though our schools of public relations varied greatly, there was a wide range of crossover, but I also have the mindset there is enough business to go around. I never viewed Celeste, nor any other publicist for that matter, as my competition. Even when I am legitimately competing with another publicist, when bidding for business, I don't worry about what another publicist is up to. Every public relations practitioner has her own unique attributes and weaknesses. I could never be the same as another publicist, and I'm certain they could never be me.

After successfully pulling off about four "Girls Night Out" events, Celeste got wind of what was going down in this quaint Haddonfield store, and rumor has it she freaked out. I'll never forget dialing into my voicemail, from my boyfriend's third bedroom where I worked most days, to retrieve a message. It was Celeste. I almost dropped the receiver when I heard her say her name. "Hi Mindie, this is Celeste, I think this situation constitutes an emergency, and you must call me back RIGHT NOW!" Was she for real? Not only was she curt in her message, but I was also pretty sure she was yelling at me from the level of volume in her voice. Hell no! Not only would I not be calling Celeste back, but I also instantly hit "delete" from the voicemail menu options and went on with my tasks.

Two weeks went by. Then, one afternoon, when I went to pick up my company mail at the local post office, where I had set up a post office box for my business, I was hit with a bombshell. As I glanced through the many letters, most of which were bills and some checks from clients, I noticed an unusual letter in the mix. It was from a law firm and had an Atlantic City address on it. I didn't recognize the name. I walked over to the post office's reception area and ripped it open. My jaw dropped. As I began to read what it said, I stood there right in the middle of the Voorhees, NJ post office in disbelief. It was about the Celeste debacle. She had hired an attorney (who I later came to find out was really her friend) to scare me. I was being accused of stealing her idea and other likeness, and they were demanding that I cease and desist any future "Girls Night Out" events. I was dumb-founded. Yes, our events bore the same name, but so did a million other gatherings all over the country, not to mention the globe. It wasn't ideal that they both were launched in the same year, but our audiences couldn't have been more different, and I certainly wasn't marketing to her clientele nor attempting to steal any of her ideas. My event wasn't even *my* event! I had been hired by the boutique owner to execute her idea for her customers. I did the legwork and came up with the event collaborators, but I certainly didn't create it.

When I returned to my home office, I immediately called my boyfriend to share the news. He was equally angry and felt badly that I was being bullied by the owner of a more established PR firm. She had a few more years under her belt owning a business, and he got the hunch that she saw me as up-and-coming competition and didn't like it. Not one bit. He enlisted his friend, a very well-known and aggressive criminal attorney, to draft a response. The attorney was kind to offer this favor and created a rash response that I found both humorous and on point. It went something like this: "Business is a fair playing field, and Miss Barnett neither stole the concept nor likeness of 'Girls Night Out'...." It went on to say how I would not be halting the event and summed up her accusations as asinine. I couldn't have agreed more. I was sure I had seen the last of this silly spat. I went on with my life and kept planning and coordinating the monthly get-togethers, along with the other mounting tasks that were consuming my calendar as my client roster grew bigger by the week. Life was good. Until it wasn't.

One crisp fall night in late October, I was facilitating another "Girls Nights Out" at the chic boutique. The featured guest had just wrapped up his talk, and the twenty-plus attendees who were the epitome of the ladies-who-lunch stereotype were laughing, chatting, and shopping. Things were moving like clockwork. My assistant and I were at the front of the store, catching our breath and making small talk as we glanced in the direction of the laughter and smiles. I was feeling content and proud and tired. Just then, the front glass door flew open, and a massive man, rough-looking and clad in a black leather jacket with a matching leather baseball hat and heavy chain belt wrapped around his thick waist, abruptly stomped in. "I'm looking for Mindie Barnett," he shouted. My eyes grew so wide I thought they may pop right out of my head. I raced to the door and instantly ushered him out, grabbing his arm and directing him onto the sidewalk. Thankfully, I had been positioned in the front of the store, so I was able to quickly whisk him out as fast as he'd come in. By the grace of God, since the store was filled with loud chatter and clatter, no one really noticed what had just happened. My client had, but at least her customers had not! Out on the sidewalk, in the dark, I confirmed, "I am Mindie Barnett." He tossed a very thick, tan envelope at my feet and pronounced, "You've been served!" I thought I was dreaming!

Looking back, I can now see how much time, money, and plotting Celeste must have given to execute this scenario. She had to have researched when my next event was, then time it out so that the server would arrive in the middle of it when the store would likely be the most crowded, and then she had to also pay the fee for the process server. This just shows how much attention Celeste had given this situation. I was so mind-boggled by it all. I, personally, had very little time to dedicate to such ridiculousness, let alone research minute details and invest funds all to anger another. At the time, I chalked it up as very odd, but realized I had a massive problem on my hands. I took the heavy packet jammed with documents into Angela's back office and gingerly placed it on her desk. I let it sit there until the event was over. I then went back out into the crowd to work. With a smile on my face, I talked calmly with the guests, happily, and let my carefree spirit shine through, despite the fact my stomach was spinning at a rapid pace. After everyone left, I helped to straighten up and get the store back in order as I always did. Then, Angela and I walked to the back office, and together we peeled back the envelope's seal and cautiously pulled out the paperwork. The material was addressed to both of us. Celeste wasn't only suing me, she was also suing Angela! OMG! I felt so bad for Angela and told her not to worry, I would handle everything, which is exactly what I did. Celeste was suing us for significant damages, and she claimed our event was hindering the progress and success of hers in Atlantic City. She claimed that her clientele might attend our event in error. In other words, if our event grew in popularity, her audience may attempt to attend our event instead. It didn't add up. But what was very apparent was that Celeste didn't want me to be in business, and this was her attempt to stop me in my tracks before I became too successful and potentially hindered her growth and prosperity. This ordeal is the perfect example of a woman competing with another woman. Her eyes were wide open, and her claws were out, freshly sharpened and ready for attack. Sadly, this sort of display is very commonplace in the workplace among women.

A 2013 *Forbes* report cites two major factors contributing to this "woman versus woman" behavior. The first is psychological. Often, when women view other women as competition, it is driven by their own insecurities. The attacker doesn't believe that her own abilities are enough to conquer her career goals, so she tries to take down anyone who may potentially block her way. She is always looking for possible threats to her success, the magazine shares. Society often teaches young girls that other women are usually out to get you, especially if you are ambitious, beautiful, and talented, so you better watch your back! And we can't ignore the everyday, simple female rivalry in the workplace either. Even in 2021, the corporate world is still male dominated, which creates the perfect storm for setting women up to compete with one another. "The psyche behind that competitive mindset coupled with the workplace culture creates the nastiest of female rivalries," explains Philadelphia-based psychologist Dr. Jaime Zuckerman. "It's plain old-fashioned jealousy. Jealousy stemming from low self-worth, insecurities in one's abilities or appearances, and a general internalized message of feeling less than. In this sense, another woman's success isn't viewed as well deserved, but rather as something that doesn't belong to them; something that is 'up for grabs,'" she says.

"Staying true to oneself and core values makes it less likely that their self-worth would be contingent on another's views or opinions. In other words, one's sense of self remains stable and within their control. A stable sense of self greatly reduces the risk of anxiety, depression, and low self-esteem. It also increases self-confidence and self-effi-cacy, or the belief in one's own abilities." Dr. Zuckerman's recipe to avoid becoming a bitch to begin with is staying connected to your core values, which also makes you more willing to learn from mistakes and improve. "When mas-tering new tasks is met with curiosity rather than fear of incompetence or avoidance, there is no need for compensa-tory strategies to make oneself feel better," says Zuckerman, who's quickly becoming a household name among women all over the country, with her daily Instagram posts of enlightenment. "[Confident women] are secure in their own skin and therefore do not perceive other women as threats."

Women are also known for notoriously being a "bitch," because unlike men, women don't compete in an outward fashion. When men compete, they don't hold back; what you see is what you get. Men will climb to the top, jockey for a promotion among their peers, and maintain an open and upfront attitude. They're not worried about percep-tion when it comes to competition. Women, on the other hand, notoriously struggle with how others view them, how they're being perceived, and, therefore, act in secretive, pas-sive ways. They will plot behind closed doors (like planning to sue their competition) with indirect aggression. Women also intentionally hide their competitive nature, which eventually manifests into full-blown ravaged "bitch-mode" because of our culture. Women are raised to be the quint-essential good girl. Women are told to be kind, and to not to be jealous of others. But when a female lacks self-confidence, self-esteem, or simple self-love, so goes the downward spiral of always looking over her shoulder and sneakily tripping the potential next best thing to keep pace in the race. "Young girls, particularly in an individualistic society like the United States, are taught at an early age to do, to be, and to look their best. This internalized message guides their behavioral choices throughout their lives. Inherent in this message is the notion that where they are currently 'at' is not good enough. They feel they must be smarter, thinner, and better looking than their peers. It's this mindset that fosters ongoing female competition against each other rather than lifting one another up and highlighting individual strengths," Dr. Zuckerman says. It's not a terrible way to be, but in business the bitchy reputation is the kiss of death. Eventually, that nasty reputation will precede all else, and no one really wants to work with or for a bitch.

Despite my belief that the lawsuit had no merit, I was still forced to hire a copyright attorney. No more lawyer favors this time. I had to pay the attorney's expensive retainer, and we began with arbitration, in an attempt to avoid going to court and racking up even more billable time I'd have to pay. The encounter was stressful and very heated. Celeste sat across a big conference table from Angela and me with her attorney while our lawyers went back and forth. She and I had very few verbal exchanges. At one point her attorney seemed to be agreeing with what my attorney was saying, and I saw her face turn a bright shade of rouge. Then, she tried to take over the session. Yelling directly at me, she said how the encounter was wasting her time. She wanted to be repaid for damages and requested a sum that would have put me into great debt and possibly debilitated the growth of my still-young company. I imagine that was her mission, and she was hell-bent on succeeding. Then, her lawyer grabbed the reins and yanked her back into reality. After speaking firmly with Celeste as she was, as he said, "out of line," she was asked to leave the room, and he handled the remainder of the arbitration without her presence. The minute the door closed behind her, the air shifted as the heavy tension seemed to dissipate. I could still see her straight, auburn-red blunt-cut hair through the floor-to-ceiling windows, but she was on the other side of them. We worked out the details, and despite the fact our attorneys both agreed the "Girls Night Out" title was indeed generic and unoriginal, my side agreed to change the name of our event so that there would be a difference. I was fine with that. So was Angela. Then, when the session ended, my attorney, Angela, and I walked out of the room and passed Celeste, and I glanced in her direction. I smirked at her and turned my head and nose slightly upward. The ordeal was over, and while neither of us really won, I still felt like the victor. She had not succeeded in shutting down my firm. She had not succeeded in rattling me enough to make me falter or cry. Although I was nervous and stressed by the situation, she didn't know that. I had shown a strong game face and all the while kept my calm, my confidence, and remained all class. I had won indeed!

Celeste and I still have never spoken, and in time the ordeal became water under the bridge, at least for me. It's not a secret that Celeste is not my favorite person, but as I mentioned before, I do have the utmost respect for her. Not because of what she attempted to do to me or for her work antics, but for the successful business that she created and eventually sold. She is a shrewd entrepreneur, and I admire her for that. I personally believe that there is enough business to go around. I don't need to steal another's client or another's idea. I trust myself, I trust the universe, and I trust my team. I believe in myself, my capabilities, and my talent.

On the other side of the spectrum is the business bond I maintain with my colleague and friend Jaimi Blackburn. Jaimi couldn't be any further from a bitch if she tried. Jaimi, an incredibly seasoned publicist based in the Philadelphia region, with a similar resume and news background to mine, is the definition of class, grace, and a true team player. She could also easily view me as negative competition, and I her, but that's not the case. Never has been and never will be! She and I met back in 2012, when I was working on a big project with the *Philadelphia Daily News*. At the time, Jaimi was representing a very chic luxury hotel brand in the city, and we met via a mutual media contact. I was helping the paper's columnist Jenice Armstrong with her annual "Sexy Singles" feature series, and Jenice wanted to use Jaimi's hotel client as the location for the big party at the culmination of the week-long spread. Sounded good to me! I also had restaurant clients we could have tapped for this party to offer them great exposure, but Jenice thought Jaimi's venue was stronger, and that was perfectly fine. I was happy to help and work with Jaimi to pull off a great event!

Jaimi invited Jenice and me to meet with her in the hotel's swanky hotspot, Bank & Bourbon, where we could enjoy a nice lunch and discuss the upcoming event. I had never met Jaimi before this, but I did know her name from various industry circles and many mutual friends in the news business. Her reputation was stellar. I had learned that she was a hard worker and very easy to get along with. Many had shared she was an innovator and always set up great stories. I also heard she was very nice and had a bubbly personality. In fact, many in the news business who worked with Jaimi and me were surprised to hear that we had never met. I often heard how similar we were in many respects and that she and I would hit it off, as we were essentially "cut from the same cloth." So, as you can imagine, I was excited for the lunch meeting, for more reasons than fleshing out the party details.

Everyone (including Jenice) was 100 percent accurate! I loved Jaimi the minute I met her. She was smart, had great ideas, and once all the event details were hammered out and we got to talking more on a personal level, she started sharing more about her background. I was impressed with her strong news experience. We exchanged our contact information with the intention of planning more collaborations in the future, possibly even referring business to one another as opportunities arose. Our collaborative event was a great one. The party was off the charts, and everyone involved couldn't have been happier. About a month after the very successful "Sexy Singles" party was wrapped, she and I met for another lunch—just the two of us this time. At that lunch, we really bonded. Jaimi shared more about her personal life, as did I. She was once divorced, newly married, and had two teenage daughters and now two teenage stepdaughters. I was recently divorced, with two young children, and just finding my way. We swapped single mom stories and shared anecdotes of enlightenment. Jaimi offered me a wealth of advice, having already gone through much of what I was just starting to encounter: navigating a new home, raising two kids as a co-parent, dating again. I really leaned in as she shared a lot of what she learned through her own trial and error. I shared stories of employee management, working in television news, and some of my unique career insight, having been on that side of the fence. She did the same regarding print journalism. She also shared that she was an adjunct public relations professor at Temple University and encouraged me to become one too, given my strong background. At the time, my schedule wouldn't allow for it, but it's definitely something I intend to pursue in the future. I still maintain ties with the public relations dean at the university, ties I attained through Jaimi's generous introduction.

Women who support other women bring impact. By raising one another up and channeling positive reinforcement and collaboration, we are united in so many ways. Dr. Zuckerman believes we all come to the table with different patterns of interacting. "Varying perspectives and inherently different life experiences and struggles are a part of our makeup. To compare ourselves to another not only means we disregard their life experiences to date, but also minimizes our own struggles. Any time self-worth is contingent on another's opinions, strength, and performance, it sets us up for failure," she warns.

Published research in the *Harvard Business Review* shows that while both male and female professionals benefit greatly from support and connectedness to their peers, women who have a core group of tight-knit, like-minded female contacts are more likely to secure executive roles with more leadership capabilities. They're also more likely to achieve higher pay scales and better benefits. Among men, the study found nothing linking their career success with their network of other men, so this collaboration appears to be more critical to the success of the female professional. The study also points out that women who are climbing the ranks into leadership often face cultural and systematic obstacles, making it more difficult for them to break the proverbial glass ceiling. Because of this, women are constantly battling a "blind prejudice." But the research shows women can overcome this is by maintaining strong female allies. When women align themselves with other women who can share experiences, they are stronger. Women who have been there, done that and who are willing to dish about their war stories to prevent a fellow female from falling into the same pitfalls are an invaluable source of strength.

Jaimi and I are exactly that to one another. She is just one example of the army of women I've aligned myself with over the years. My mind and my arms are always open. My mantra is to help and give of myself without expecting anything in return. I live by the mindset of karma. I know that if you pass good onto others, good will return to you. It's that simple. Be a good friend, a good employer, a strong employee, and a kind-hearted human being and positive prosperity will come. It always does. Without fail. It takes a strong spirit to stand by these values, especially when life throws out curveballs. It's easy to take the high road when the path is smooth and the vision ahead is clear. But when the tide is turbulent and the light seems dim, not so much. However, it's in these times of real trial when staying the course and not deviating from your integrity matters the most. Dr. Zuckerman agrees. "It takes one's self worth and places the responsibility on another to manage it, which ultimately results in feeling out of control regarding self-esteem. Their success and productivity are often attributed to luck or external variables, while their failures are due to inherent flaws and the belief that self-derived improvement is not possible," she shares.

We are often critical of other women when we feel bad about ourselves. Experts say that in comparing ourselves to others, we create a scenario that makes us feel inferior. In choosing not to compare yourself to other women, you'll be supporting your own well-being and mindset, putting you in a better position to support others as well. In addition, comparison can eventually compromise your capability to grow. If done too often and repeatedly, it can become an obsessive addiction and create a dangerous downward spiral. Much of these ill-fated comparison antics are played out on social media. It's so easy to spend hours combing through another's photos on Facebook or Instagram, looking at what other women have created and achieved, feeling sick and depressed afterwards about where you personally may be. But this is an utter waste of time! What an unproductive way to spend even a minute of your life. This exercise will only lead to negativity and destructive beliefs.

"It is a rarity in the world of social media for people to post their first selfie attempt, uncropped and filter-less. Why? Those types of images do not get noticed as much," Dr. Zuckerman shares. "Remember, the goal of most social media is not to just show off your latest meal, but rather to elicit some sort of acknowledgment via likes, comments, and shares. The fundamental issue with social media comparison is that comparison image is simply not realistic. Social media is a snapshot, literally, of people's lives. A perfectly curated, cropped, and filtered image of a life the poster wants to project to the world. When these comparisons occur, the use of these enhancers are often glossed over and not taken into consideration."

Some of the feelings following social media indulgence include feeling not as rich, not as beautiful, not as smart, not as lovable, and not as successful as the woman you may be trailing on social media. "Often, the assumption is made that a post is a direct reflection of the poster's daily life, a life of constant smiles, healthy relationships, and limited, if not a total absence of, personal struggles. This 'good vibes only' message can be significantly detrimental to the self-esteem and self-worth of their followers. Comparison to what appears to be a life of constant beauty, health, and happiness is setting a person up for failure. The follower is routinely falling short of unrealistic expectations, feeling as if she can't measure up to a particular standard and is in some way deficient," explains Dr. Zuckerman.

At the heart of the comparison dance, and the eye of the storm, when it comes to women snuffing out other women in business, it all boils down to lack of confidence. Feelings of inadequacy and a lack of self-worth are always at the forefront of the comparison game. Why do women search and search just to feel a pang in their chest? Experts say the answer is easy. The social media stalkers are on the hunt for validation. They are seeking anything to reinforce their own belief that they're "not enough." They compare and sometimes lash out on another female on their path, but who they really loathe is themselves. It's a very sad and vicious cycle. That's the bitch's deepest and darkest secret revealed.

While comparison is an internal cognitive process in which we compare aspects of ourselves to our *perceptions* of these same aspects of another, "Comparison can be dangerous to our self-esteem. Comparing oneself to another assumes that both people begin on equal footing. For example, comparing your grade on an exam to another student's score excludes several variables (i.e., learning disabilities, amount of sleep the night prior to the exam, amount of studying, test anxiety)," says Dr. Zuckerman. "Comparing oneself to another is a slippery slope. No two people are ever truly starting on an even playing field, with each having different experiences and abilities. Moreover, because self-comparison is contingent on our perceptions of another, we give up control of our self-worth by placing it in the hands of another."

Jaimi and I have always compared our lives, but in a healthy and uplifting way. Experts say that kind of comparison is much needed. When comparison is not obsessive and instead used as inspiration for one's own journey, it is positive reinforcement. There is a huge difference in energy, and even outcome, when another person's success is used as a vision to emulate rather than in a self-demoralizing way. The "positive vibe" comparison can spark a fire from within. When you see another conquer a quest, it can push you to set a higher goal for yourself. Healthy comparison entails looking upward after a role model who is ahead on her career path, providing a blueprint for how to get there. Healthy comparison uses another's expansion as a reminder that similar outcomes are attainable for you too, and that greatness is on the horizon.

"Competition can be both healthy and detrimental depending on the circumstances," Dr. Zuckerman says. "Healthy competition involves a person wanting to better their existing abilities or push themselves outside their comfort zone. The need to better oneself is internally driven." She gives the example of competing in a tennis match as a form of healthy competition. "However, competing against another out of jealousy or a need to always be 'better' than them can be damaging. If the effort to be better is driven by jealousy or fear, that effort is more likely to reflect unhealthy behaviors."

Jaimi and I have grown closer as years have passed. I've met and become very good friends with her husband, Ron. I've met her children, and she's met mine. She attended my adult Bat Mitzvah, I attended the *shiva* for her father's funeral, and she has referred more prospective clients to my PR firm than I can count. Jaimi hosted me when I launched my first book, *Intermission*, at one of her clients' swanky waterfront Philadelphia restaurants, The Mosholu. I will never forget the incredible night she created for me. It was full of glitz and glamour and boasted a huge spread of cocktails and light bites. The party was widely covered by the press, equally beneficial to both her and me, and was very well attended. I was so touched and incredibly grateful. As I write this book now, she and I are brainstorming another amazing launch party for the fall of 2021. Knowing Jaimi, I'm sure that book bash will be even more successful than the first! She is a gem and the type of female friend anyone would want in their corner. She is confident, she doesn't peer over her shoulder, worried who's coming down the pike, and she lets her "competition" shine bright. Another's glow doesn't make your shine less brilliant. So, never unscrew another's lightbulb! Only a bitch would do that!

Don't Be a Bitch Bullets #8

Maneuvering Around a Mean Girl

✓ *Figure out what she's doing to press your buttons. Once you've pinpointed what the bitch in your life does that most makes you mad, you'll have a handle on your emotions and be able to regain control.*

✓ *Try to slip into her (Prada) shoes. See if you can see the situation from her point of view. Perhaps there is something you are doing that set her off unintentionally.*

✓ *Disarm her. Talk to her face-to-face in a neutral location. Acknowledge the tension and maturely see if you can come to a resolution.*

✓ *Keep cool. Calm is key. Calm will make you look professional and polished and calm will keep her in crazy town.*

✓ *Seek support. Don't go on a rant or try and throw anyone under the bus; seeking help from a superior in an effort to obtain advice is productive and will be viewed in a high regard.*

Chapter 9

BUH-BYE, BITCH!

"I'm not a tough boss in that I don't raise my voice, I don't freak out, and I don't have a temper most of the time."

–Rachel Zoe

*T*ry as you may (and God knows I have certainly tried when a bitch out of hell is tossed in my direction), sometimes you just need to turn up your nose, snap your head in the opposite direction, and tell that bitch to "talk to the hand." Sometimes the best thing you can give to a bitch is your silence. When you're working for one, that may be easier said than done, but when they're in your life as a client, a friend, or the worst kind of all, a frenemy, you can close the door and bolt it shut. Without blinking an eye. No amount of money nor personal perks will ever be worth more than your sanity, peace, and pride.

I am happy to say that my dealings with such "devils" have been few and far between. But I have had some doozies to deal with and have learned how to stay true to myself, maintain my sophistication, and end the union with finesse. Just because you may be dealing with a tornado doesn't mean you need to mirror that bad behavior. Rise above so that when push comes to shove, no one will ever be able to say you're less. And you'll leave with more of yourself and your mind, which is vital in running a company!

In 2009 I was hired by a former client's ex-husband to lead a PR campaign for his feline fashion empire. We'll call it Purrfectly Pretty. The brand had about five locations in the Greater Philadelphia vicinity with plans to expand into other cities soon. The company was impressive. The President, Alex, had very deep pockets and, therefore, the ability to travel overseas to acquire the finest in fur baby accessories at a fraction of what it would typically cost to order wholesale in the US. Because he also had the resources to personally make the trip and not just trust ordering online, the merchandise looked and felt like it was top dollar. But it wasn't, and people loved that about Purrfectly Pretty. At first, I was hesitant to even take the initial meeting when Alex called me. His now ex-wife had been the one to hire me when they were married, and I still had fond feelings for her. I also knew how horrible their divorce had been, especially for her, as she walked away essentially penniless and left the pet company they had worked on and built together in his hands. But business is business, and I told myself I'd maintain a very "strictly work" demeanor at all times. This meant I wouldn't engage in much small talk, nor utter his ex-wife's name or whereabouts if ever asked.

When I went to the store's headquarters to meet with Alex and his new CEO, a woman he shared he was personally involved with, I didn't know what to expect. I knew Alex was a witty entrepreneur but also had a mean streak and wasn't the most standup of people. But when I met his new girlfriend, Elena, who would be my direct contact for all public relations-related dealings, I felt a pit in my stomach. To say Elena didn't event attempt to be kind would be an understatement. She wasn't rude or disrespectful, but I instantly had the sneaking suspicion that she did not like me. I couldn't tell you why. I had been my usual bubbly self in our meeting, complete with an onslaught of stellar ideas to garner great press for her kitty kingdom. She was receptive and seemed excited to get started, but I felt a cold shoulder from her the entire time. Perhaps she was resentful that her boyfriend hired his ex-wife's publicist and that the ex-wife and I remained on good terms and were still acquaintances. I'll never know, but that was the only feasible reason I could think of.

As the campaign got underway, we were quickly able to secure a great deal of press: a "Fox Fursday" segment featuring fun Halloween costumes for Fluffy and friends and a health-skewed newspaper feature focusing on the best pet foods on the market and what your cat needs daily for the best nutrition based on breed, size, and weight. We also did a fun event called "Santa Paws" where Saint Nick posed with the felines for a small donation made to the company's sister nonprofit, an adoption organization. I loved the account, despite dealing with Elena. It was easy to pitch and fun to execute. The media loved covering the company, and because I had represented the brand once before, I was comfortable with organizing much of the media coverage without a lot of involvement from management. Namely I didn't have to deal with Elena that much. That was a blessing. But every so often, she'd reach out to me, just to press a button or two and try and rattle the press opportunity I was in the midst of facilitating. I couldn't understand why. It was as though she was trying to sabotage her own success. It was very strange indeed.

Then one day, we finally had it out. I was in the process of organizing the secured media coverage for an adopt-a-thon event Purrfectly Pretty was hosting when it became evident that something on the inside wasn't right. The media station that was given an exclusive to cover the story and film some of the nonprofit's push to have pets adopted and raise funds for their cause needed specific details before the shoot day. They wanted to know how much money had been raised to date, what the funds had recently benefited, some details about a recent project the nonprofit completed, and more. I had given Elena the producer's questions more than a week before the shoot day, and she still was uncooperative in sharing anything of importance. After various unanswered emails, I called her cell, texted her, and tried to communicate through Alex, but to no avail. Something felt off to me. I'm not saying the nonprofit's mission was not legitimate, but I didn't understand why Elena was obviously ignoring the producer's questions and my outreach. Then, at 9 p.m. the night before the shoot, she finally called me back. She was furious! She didn't care that the segment was in jeopardy if the information was not provided. She wasn't going to answer the producer's probes, and that was that. No explanation. No reasoning. Nothing. Her answer to me was to, "Make it happen." And then she hung up the phone. What the hell?

I had a longstanding relationship with this producer and his station. I considered him a friend and valued the integrity of our relationship. I also identified myself as a journalist and understood the significance of the information he sought. It was an ethics issue. I got it. I also knew that Elena was being unreasonable. I was not going to throw her or any client under the proverbial bus, but I was also not about to jeopardize my reputation with this station. I cancelled the segment. I didn't share with the producer how difficult Elena was being nor how unprofessional it was of her not to disclose the facts and accommodate his request. Instead, I said I was unable to obtain what he needed and understood the necessity of the information, therefore, I thought it was best for the station to scrap the whole thing. When I called Elena early the next morning to share the news and my decision to nix the segment, she went berserk! She screamed and cursed and called me pretty much every name in the book (all but the nice ones!) and insulted me for my so-called naïve mindset in abiding by the rules of the station. I listened, having prepared myself for her tirade, but still was shocked by the way she conducted herself. I tried to just listen until she was nearing the end of her harangue and then calmly said goodbye and hung up the phone. Then I opened my laptop and drafted an email to Alex and copied Elena. I resigned. I was within my right to do so, per my contract, as we clearly didn't see eye-to-eye and I was now viewing the account, due to Elena's conduct, as a liability for my company. But even more than that, I saw Elena for what she really was. A bitch. And it was time to say buh-bye.

An August 2018 *Byron Magazine* feature explores seven ways to deal with difficult people. The author referenced the drama triangle, first coined by psychiatrist Dr. Stephen Karpman, as a key way to explain most dysfunctional relating. The triangle includes the archetypes of persecutor, rescuer, and victim. If you fall into one of these roles, he says you're fueling drama into your life. Unfortunately, there is no escaping getting swept up into this relationship triangle indefinitely. *Byron Magazine* quotes Karpman as saying we have all been sucked into it at some point in our lives. The components are interchangeable too, which means that at one point or another, we have all been in each. But all three spots feed and perpetuate each other, thus creating drama. Those involved create misery for themselves and for others. The only exit from this insanity is to step up and be a responsible relator. Not exactly a small pill to swallow, especially when dealing with a personality like Elena's!

When dealing with volatile scenarios and complicated people, the goal is to walk away from a disagreement and feel good about how you maneuvered it, not because you won. I certainly didn't win when I cancelled the segment I had pitched a month prior. I also didn't win by resigning from a high-paying client contract. But I did manage to maintain my dignity, inner calm, and didn't lose much sleep over it, so in essence that's a victory. And according to the *Byron Magazine* article, I scored high.

Experts stress by winning, you're simply walking away and feeling good. If you cannot avoid reacting (and respond instead), erupting, or lowering yourself to engage with the culprit, or in my case, the bitch, you will undeniably regret it. You could permanently dismantle a professional or personal relationship and fall prey to gossip about *your* "bitchy" behavior too. This notion also applies to narcissists in the workplace, irritating in-laws, or an up-and-coming young office talent vying for your desk. Also, an excruciatingly difficult ex. It's always the best bet to remain calm, responsive, and clear when dealing with problematic people. It's more powerful and will prove to be productive for everyone involved.

Karpman says there are seven tactics to take when dealing with trying people. The first is to know you're not the "fixer." It's not your job nor issue to mend what is wrong with another's life. You can only control you and are only responsible for your own actions. As my tween children would say, "Stay out of their business." Next, pick your presence, and by that, experts say the existence you bring to a situation will either magnify it or diminish it. When you bring peace and clarity to a heated situation, you can reconstruct it. When you put revenge on the backburner and come with an open mind, you'll find your muscles. The best and most effective way to approach another with ease, when what you really want to do is punch them in the face, is to treat each salty encounter as an opportunity to continue to train your mind to be inquisitive.

Another sure way to beat the odds of dealing with a bitch is to understand the reality of their disposition. As we explored in Chapter 8, it's likely they're combating a distorted belief system and possibly have built up hatred or fear. Something inside them is emotionally off-kilter. It's not really you they're after, they just don't know how to relate to their own insecurities, or how to heal from their life disappointments and feelings of inadequacy. The most powerful act you can do in these circumstances is to do nothing at all. Free yourself and spare yourself from unnecessary grief. The inaction doesn't mean you're weak or accepting the other's poor behavior, it simply shows your strength and ability not to succumb to another's put-downs, irrational dialogue, or nastiness. And as with any toxic relationship, it's crucial you set solid boundaries. Don't be afraid to cut another off, whether it's a work, romantic, or family relationship. When drama ensues, you need not engage and waste your precious energy on someone irrational. Joining another's drama club, just because they're in need of attention or wish to throw their negative emotions on your lap, is beneath you. Love yourself enough and have enough respect for your well-being to shut them down.

Choice is power. You always have a choice. A choice about how you react: do you lose your cool and lash out, or respond and speak calm and collected? Do you stay true and listen to the unruly person rant and flip out in a deranged demeanor, or do you join in and strike up a screaming match? Sometimes you need to act. Some situations don't go away on their own. But how you make your move speaks volumes. About three years ago, my firm was contracted by another public relations firm in New York City. I had gained the attention of a Manhattan plastic surgeon. He wanted me to handle his consumer public relations, and the publicist who was already working with him and handling his industry-specific business-to-business media strategy was irate. She didn't want to hire me, out of fear that if he did, he might wind up working one-on-one with me, which meant that she'd lose control. She likely feared that he might opt to have my firm handle the entire campaign and she'd be out of a client. She didn't share that with me, of course, but based on her tone when we spoke and her overall demeanor, I'd bet money on it. Her name was Sylvia, and she was about twenty years my senior. She had an award-winning PR firm with a large staff and a big city attitude to boot. I liked her at first, despite the rough way she introduced herself when she reached out to me. "Hi, Mindie. This is Sylvia Masterson. My client, Doctor Rosen, wanted me to contact you. He is interested in doing more consumer news and would like me to work with you." It's not what she said. It's the way she said it. Cold. Rash. Aggravated. But I didn't care. I knew I was good at my job and that I'd be able to get Dr. Rosen a lot of media coverage. I knew I'd make her look good, since she was requesting her firm hire mine, not the doctor's office. And I also knew that I am a people person. I'd be kind and hardworking, and she would be forced to love me. That was my plan. And it worked.

About six weeks into the contract, Dr. Rosen had been on the nationally syndicated television program *Inside Edition*; he was featured on WPIX11 in New York City; and he had an upcoming ABC7 shoot on the horizon. He was happy and Sylvia was too. All was great. In fact, it was so good, Sylvia requested that I meet her in person at her office on the Upper East Side to discuss other accounts she was interested in hiring me to help her with. Over lunch, one early spring afternoon, we chatted in her conference room about some of the other medical companies she worked with and thought I could support her with. We discussed what all that would entail and carved out several other contract terms. Things were looking up. Sylvia was my new best friend.

After much aggravation, the ABC7 story had finally been executed. But what should have been about five hours of work to set up the segment turned into about twenty, all of which I couldn't bill for, since we were engaged in an all-inclusive monthly retainer, which is the way I typically do business. I usually end up getting short-changed in the end, but it makes for less of a bookkeeping headache for me. Some of the major hiccups included the doctor office's unwillingness to secure a patient to profile. Sylvia also refused to help. At the time, my firm was just breaking into the New York City market, so our contacts with anyone other than clients and press were still developing. So, we were on our own to secure a "patient" to travel to New York City and have filler injected. The story was about the uptick of millennials looking to do what was being coined pre-juvenation—trying to freeze the clock before signs of aging appeared. Sylvia promised that if we paid the patient's travel expenses, she would reimburse us with the next invoice. I was fine with that. The shoot for the story went off smoothly and everyone, including the patient, was happy. Then, a few weeks went by, and the story aired. It was strong and garnered a great deal of buzz for Dr. Rosen. I sent the online link of the piece to Sylvia and her team to document and share with the doctor, but I never heard back. I got busy, and the fact that my email went without a reply didn't immediately register. But about two days later, I recalled never hearing from Sylvia. In the past, and it is standard with other clients, after sharing a press clip, prompt feedback usually follows. So, I emailed her again to follow up. Still nothing. Then, I looked at the calendar and realized her payment for that month was overdue. Now I was concerned, so I called her. The call went to voicemail. I reached out again the next morning and got her voicemail again. I rang back, this time asking for her assistant. After listening to one full song on hold, her assistant, Maryanne, picked up and transferred me to Sylvia, who actually picked up the phone. My intention was simply to seek her feedback from the ABC7 segment and then confirm that she had mailed out my payment. But I never had a chance to speak because once she picked up the call, she started speaking to me in a very heated tone, barely taking a breath. I couldn't fully grasp what she was so angry about. I spoke to her calmly, still confused about what she was trying to convey. But my tone only triggered her more. I wound up having to extricate myself and told her I was going to hang up, since we were unable to communicate effectively and suggested we speak later that day or the next day, when we could have a conversation with clarity. She slammed the phone down before I was finished. The next day, Sylvia texted me, which is not the form of communication I prefer in business, especially when communicating important information. She shared that Dr. Rosen had fired her and that she would not be paying that month's invoice. She acknowledged that I had done a superior job and was not the reason she was fired. She said that she wasn't getting paid by the doctor, and so I wouldn't be getting paid either. I reminded her that while I sympathized, my contract was with her, not Dr. Rosen. I had rendered my services for the month, and I needed to be paid. My response sparked an inferno in Sylvia, who essentially shared she didn't care about our contract and that she had made the decision she would not be paying me. She didn't try to end the call after that pronouncement; instead she opted to continue repeating herself, reminding me that she had been in business twice as long as I had and that she held the power. I listened. I didn't react. I didn't even reply. I hung up and called my firm's attorney. I then filed a complaint against her and within a week, I received a check with Sylvia's signature. I stayed on the high road but held my own and remained strong. I also got my hard-earned money. I lost the doctor's account but gained so much more. Myself!

You can choose to spread chaos or calm in your wake as you move through life. When tossed a tragedy like an unruly bitch, you can sink or swim. If you choose to look at each unfortunate encounter to learn and grow, much like a mistake, you'll gain the power. It's the power of choice. When dealing with conflict, remind yourself of this personal pact. The promise to stay the course, keep your cool, and err on the side of kindness always. When we don't let go, grudges and grievances ultimately blend into our personalities. The feelings of anger and bitterness are addictive. The two can strengthen the ego and give us the façade of having power, but it's smoke and mirrors. Dealing with difficult people is an ongoing life lesson. The more you experience, the better you'll be at smiling, shutting the door, and saying, "Buh-bye, Bitch!"

Don't Be a Bitch Bullets #9

Keeping your Calm

✓ *Don't take it personally. A bitchy colleague or boss may be depressed or dealing with drama at home. If they snap, don't assume it's about you.*

✓ *Prepare a plan. Before confronting the culprit, identify your reasons for the discussion. Setting intentions will dictate whether the conversation will be a pass or fail.*

✓ *Welcome confrontation. Yes, actually welcome it! Invite the problematic person out for coffee or seek a deeper conversation at the office to try and ease the tension. Hear them out and be open to accepting you may unintentionally be the root of the problem.*

✓ *Write it down. Document everything that is troublesome. Keep a calendar noting the dates when nasty remarks were made. File emails, don't delete text messages, and even save voicemail messages. You may need the material as evidence, if you decide to take your complaints to the next level.*

✓ *Drop it. There's a difference between behavior that impacts your ability to live or work with someone and a personality trait that just annoys you. When a coworker crosses the line into the bully lane, it's time to go to management or human resources.*

Chapter 10

KINDNESS CAN EQUAL CASH

"Real integrity is doing the right thing, knowing that nobody's going to know whether you did it or not."

–Oprah Winfrey

I have come a long way since starting MB and Associates PR nearly two decades ago in my parents' spare bedroom in Southern New Jersey. At the time, I was an out-of-work TV reporter killing time between jobs and fully expected that I would soon go back to work in news. But after signing my very first clients and falling madly in love with the public relations field and the power that it has to shape perceptions, I have discovered that this is my true passion. It has paid off tremendously for me both professionally and personally. I am literally living the dream and am successful beyond what I ever expected. I don't take any of my success for granted and am well aware that if I ever get too complacent, the success can disappear in a flash. There are times when I am patiently coaching a client through his first on-air appearance or excitedly helping a major company develop a new communication strategy that I pinch myself as a reminder that this is really my life. I get to use the skills I honed all those years working in TV stations in Champaign, Illinois, and Monroe, Louisiana, to help my clients increase their visibility and grow their businesses.

MB and Associates is headquartered in a glamourous two-story loft-style condominium in Marlton, New Jersey that I proudly purchased all by myself and will one day hand down to my two precious children. It is outfitted with gorgeous crystal chandeliers in every room, dark hardwood floors, and plush designer rugs. The walls are covered with headshots of my team members and framed press clippings from *The Wall Street Journal, Harper's Bazaar, The New York Times* and other publications that we have gotten for our clients. I also have a life-sized photo of me on the cover of my first book, *Intermission: How Fervor, Friendships and Faith Took Me to the Second Act,* and various promotional signage from the book tour on display. The walls of my personal office are painted my favorite blush pink color. In the center of it all is my custom-designed glass desk that makes me feel very inspired. Walking into this magnificent space pumps me up each morning as I begin to work that day's magic.

Several years ago, we opened our second location in New York City in the Financial District to better service our clients located in the New York region. MB and Associates shares this huge, impressive space that overlooks the city skyline at 55 Broad Street with Bold Worldwide. I look forward to staffing it full-time in the near future with an employee who I have been grooming. I split my time between the suburban New Jersey home I share with my two children and two adorable dogs and my stylish, single-girl apartment in a luxury high-rise building on the Upper East Side. It is conveniently located not far from where many of my clients and friends are situated. NYC's Fox5 and ABC television stations also are easily accessible from there.

I could not be prouder of MB and Associates' many accomplishments. It has grown from having just a few shop owners on its roster to representing major healthcare institutions, Fortune 500 companies, and leading business professionals. We have extensive contacts with local outlets in cities all over the country and national media. Our clients regularly appear on network or nationally syndicated TV shows such as the *Dr. Oz Show, The Tamron Hall Show, ABC's Good Morning America, Inside Edition, Fox & Friends, HLN, the BCC,* and nationally acclaimed print publications like *The Wall Street Journal* and *The New York Times*, among other outlets. I've had the pleasure of working with big-time celebrities such as Grammy Award winner Paula Abdul, former Philadelphia Eagles defensive back Tra Thomas, Pitbull collaborator Montana Tucker, nationally known psychotherapist Dr. Robi Ludwig, and broadcast news legend NBC *The Today Show's* Sheinelle Jones, among many others. Many of these incredible people I also call friends. That's the best part of all!

Along the way, I have mentored dozens of young, talented public relations practitioners who have gone on to work for places such as the Pennsylvania Attorney General's Office, or even started their own firms. I consider their success to be my success as well. Part of my mission in this life is to share some of things that I've learned along the way. I wrote *You Don't Need to Be a Bitch to Be a Boss* to help business owners and managers learn from some of my mistakes so they won't have to experience the struggles that I did. One of the biggest things I hope people can take away from me is that being kind is good business. You get much better results from employees when you lead with thoughtfulness and love than with bitchiness. As I've shared, over the years, I've worked for many bosses who believed just the opposite. They thought that being a hard-ass with me and my colleagues would translate to better results. Wrong! I did not perform well under those circumstances. I was never loyal to those bosses. If I have that mindset, then I'm sure others do as well. When you're managing people, you not only hurt yourself by acting like a bitch, but you're not helping the people under you either. You're not inspiring your employees to be better people. You're not doing all you can to improve your company's bottom line. There's no good that comes from that kind of negativity. It's not healthy to walk around like some mean old witch.

One of the things that I learned from managing my team remotely during the COVID-19 pandemic is the importance of adopting a more zen-like mindset. When I am centered, calm, and focused on the positive, I make better decisions. I am more responsive as opposed to reactive. I also sleep better. I have more energy. I have more spark when I pitch potential stories to the news media. I get more excited about going after prospective clients. That's why I try and meditate most mornings for ten minutes. I do it with an app. I light a candle. I drink my coffee. I listen to the person on the meditation app through my earbuds linked to my phone. I try and workout too, because I'm a big believer in exercising for stress relief. It always puts me in a better mood and gives me more energy for the day. I fill my diffuser with essential oils and meditate at the end of the day as well, when my schedule allows. It helps me control my mind so that I remain present. It stops me from dwelling on what I might have done wrong that day and worrying about the future. I am present and that helps me stay grounded. During the day, I keep a lighted candle at my desk. It makes me feel a little bit more at peace in what can be a very hectic environment. I have a crystal on my desk to promote the flow of good energy. All of these things help me stay centered so that when I'm writing a press release or drafting a pitch, I'm fully focused.

The universe will help you reach any goal you set for yourself, but you have to pay attention to the signs it gives you. That might come in the form of a feather you notice lying on the ground as you're walking or something else that has some sort of meaning to you. Only you can determine what that is. As a boss, take responsibility for your own life but also take responsibility for the life you share with your employees. Worry about more than just your bottom line. Make a point of caring about your employees. Whether they are part-time or salaried, full-time team members, you have a responsibility to them almost as much as you do to your clientele to give them a good experience and give them something that they can use as a stepping-stone to something either inside or outside your company. Make their time with you a positive life experience. Not every boss does that. They don't necessarily enable their team to have such experiences. They're narrow-minded about making money. My advice is for you to give of yourself. Your employees are trusting you with their time, their mind, their talent. Don't abuse the faith they have placed in you. That does not mean that you should be a pushover. I make a point of being nice but also firm. Recently, after a year of basically working from home because of COVID-19, an employee asked if she could get a flex day once a week to continue working from home, since the office was reopening at full-time capacity. As the president of MB and Associates, I split my time between our New Jersey and New York City offices. I don't stay home just because I want to relax for a day each week. I turned down that employee's request with barely a second thought. You will not be able to make your employees happy all the time. That's unrealistic.

You should, however, take the time to get to know your employees and to learn about what their goals are. I want you to respect your employees. And I want you to care about your employees. Not just your employees as employees but your employees as people. Because once you do and you nurture them, they will give back so much more than you could ever expect. I have an employee at MB who isn't quite up to par, but she gives back so much. She is always the last one in the office every night, and she's the first one there in the morning. I'm really good to her, and she cares a lot about me and the company. That's not a relationship to be taken lightly. That's why when I introduce her and my other employees, I don't tell people that they work *for* me. I say they work *with* me. There's a big difference, and I want them to know that. I urge you to take a similar approach. Be strong. Be kind. Make smart choices. Be mindful. Be nurturing. Don't bark orders at your workers. If you can give people in your office your time, that is more valuable than almost anything. I was molded in that way, so I give back in that way. It's the right way to be. It's the right way to do business. Not to be overly spiritual, but I feel like God is always watching us. We all have a role to fill on this Earth. I want to please God. I want to do what is right in His eyes. If you are reading this book, I know you want to do the right thing as well. Wanting to be a good person and wanting to treat your employees well means you are practically there already.

When I'm making choices, I ask myself, "Is this something I would want my daughter to do? Is this something that I would be proud of if she did it?" If you don't have a child, you can substitute another special family member. I try to make the right choices to be a good person. Given everything America is experiencing, we need more people willing to work across racial and political lines and class lines and to be kind to each other. We're human beings. We need to care about one another. It doesn't matter what your age is. It doesn't matter what your skin color is. It doesn't matter what your religion is or what your sexual orientation is. We're all *people*. Skin is skin. Love is love. God is love.

Yes, this is a book about leadership and managing people, but it is also about being the best version of yourself that you can possibly be. I could have done all sorts of things—stolen a client from somebody else or maybe cut a corner a little bit with someone paying me to represent them—but

I'm proud to say that I never have and never will. I always try to do the right thing. Along the way, I have managed to become successful beyond my wildest dreams, and you can too by leading with kindness and never forgetting that you don't need to be a bitch to be a boss!

Cashing in on Kindness!

- ✓ *Be a friend. Camaraderie builds rapport and builds longevity. Being a friend goes deeper than just casual small talk. It takes time, it takes effort, and it takes energy, but it will pay off tenfold in the long run.*

- ✓ *Be authentic. Clients would much rather know you don't know than see you pretend to be something you are not. Being authentic builds trust, and trust creates lasting relationships.*

- ✓ *Be there. Be reliable. And be consistent. Answer emails and phone calls in a timely manner. Always deliver when you promise and always step up when you're late—this proves you are worthy and someone your clients can count on.*

- ✓ *Think ahead. Solve your clients' problems. Their problems are your problems, and their business should be your passion as well.*

- ✓ *Superior service—always offer it. Over-deliver, and be happy to go the extra mile to help your customers out. Even when an issue isn't under your umbrella of expertise, helping to locate the necessary support and save your customer a mistake or a setback is all in a day's work.*

ACKNOWLEDGMENTS

I would first like to thank my speaking coach, friend, and client Tricia Brouk, for planting the seed in my mind to write this second book. I had no intention of taking on another massive writing project after *Intermission* was published, but she urged me to do so, saying that I had more stories to share and that if left unsaid, I was doing an injustice to others. She was so right, and going through the process of authoring another book, I have fallen even more in love with writing as I see my skills sharpen with each strike of the keyboard.

I am sincerely grateful to my two-time publisher and confidant, Anthony Ziccardi, of Post Hill Press for obliging me and taking on my second book. I have a deep admiration for Anthony, not only because of his intelligence and experience, but also for the many talks we share, switching back and forth between the roles of mentor and mentee. He has become a dear friend, and I cherish him very much. I hope I make him half as proud of me as I am of him!

Thank you to the many MB and Associates interns and employees, past and present, for entrusting me with yourself, giving of yourself to better my company, and for your time and attention to soak up whatever information and experiences I had to offer you. You continue to make me proud, and even more rewarding than being a celebrated publicist is watching you grow and spread your own wings. I love to watch you fly!

Thank you to my many, many mentors. There are too many to name, but whether I've relished being in your shadow for a short time or a lifetime, I am forever grateful. My wish is to pay your gifts forward. Thank you to Rick Williams, Allison Gibson, Janet Zappala, Jaimi Blackburn, and Jenna Stark for taking time out of your busy lives to speak with me as I interviewed you for this book. You all amaze me, and I am honored to not only call you "mentors" but "friends" too.

I am so appreciative of Dr. Jaime Zuckerman's valuable input as she helped me digest the ins and outs of why women compete. I am blessed to serve as her very proud publicist and more than grateful for her love and support today and every day.

Thank you to my Post Hill Press editor Allie Woodlee for her encouragement, wit of words, and keen eye to fine-tune grammar and punctuation. She definitely made this book better than it was before she touched it! Thank you, also, to Maddie Sturgeon, of Post Hill Press, who once again helped me navigate the road of publishing!

There will never be enough words to express my deep and sincere gratitude to my colleague and friend Jenice Armstrong. She helped me in immeasurable ways as I wrote and pieced this book together. Through her talented editing, long Zoom strategy sessions, and ongoing input, she made this book what it is. I could never have juggled running my business, managing a crazy working-from-home climate while homeschooling my two children, and writing this book in less than five months without her. She is all that and more to me! Jenice is a dear friend I met while working for Queen Bee, and she is the greatest gift I was granted from that volatile work experience. I cannot wait to watch her soar as she embarks on an exciting new second career authoring books herself!

And last but certainly not least, I'd like to thank my very first mentors, my parents: Rick and Sandy Barnett and my youngest mentors, my children: Arielle and Julian Lichterman. My mom and dad gave me the courage and strength to live life to its fullest, never be afraid to take a chance, and to always work hard, no matter what. My children teach me to take a beat, take a breath, and enjoy life in the present. I love you all with everything I have and will forever be grateful for you—the four greatest gifts God has ever bestowed upon me!

ABOUT THE AUTHOR

*A*fter ten years working as a television news reporter and anchor within the Philadelphia and New York regions—among other cities—Mindie Barnett decided to use her knowledge and experience in the media to help propel businesses and position companies as thought-leaders. Barnett founded MB and Associates in 2003 and swiftly garnered a great deal of clients in a short amount of time. Because of her vast knowledge of the news business and strong ties with key members of the media—both on local and national levels—MB and Associates was able to achieve rapid results and obtain countless press opportunities for clients. Due to these attributes, Mindie Barnett is now one of the nation's most sought-after and respected publicists.

Mindie Barnett's public relations credits include landing clients' opportunities on *Oprah, the Today show, Good Morning America, Inside Edition, Live with Kelly and Ryan, Dr. Oz, The Doctors, Anderson Cooper 360, In Touch Weekly, US Weekly, InStyle magazine, USA Today,* and *MSNBC,* among numerous regional inclusions. Barnett was named "Business Owner of the Year," by the South Jersey chapter of the National Association of Women Business Owners. Her firm has won "Best PR Firm" by *South Jersey Biz magazine* two years in a row.

Mindie maintains her public relations and social media firm and is also the author of the self-help motivational memoir *Intermission,* a keynote speaker, the host of *The Race for the Ring* podcast, and an on-air television contributor. Mindie is the mother of two and resides in Manhattan.